Leadership in Energy and Environmental Design

LEED®
GA
Practice Exams

Green Associate

David M. Hubka, DE, LEED AP

The Power to Pass
www.ppi2pass.com

Professional Publications, Inc. • Belmont, California

LEED® and USGBC® are registered trademarks of the U.S. Green Building Council. PPI® is not affiliated with the U.S. Green Building Council (USGBC) or the Green Building Certification Institute (GBCI), and does not administer the LEED AP program or LEED Green Building Rating System. PPI does not claim any endorsement or recommendation of its products or services by USGBC or GBCI.

Energy Star® (ENERGY STAR®) is a registered trademark of the U.S. Environmental Protection Agency (EPA).

Also available for the LEED exams at **www.ppi2pass.com/LEED**:

LEED Prep GA: What You Really Need to Know to Pass the LEED Green Associate Exam
LEED GA Flashcards: Green Associate
LEED O&M Practice Exam: Operations & Maintenance
LEED Prep O&M: What You Really Need to Know to Pass the LEED AP Operations & Maintenance Exam
LEED O&M Flashcards: Operations & Maintenance

LEED GA PRACTICE EXAMS: GREEN ASSOCIATE

Current printing of this edition: 1

Printing History

edition number	printing number	update
1	1	New book.

Printed in the United States of America

PPI
1250 Fifth Avenue, Belmont, CA 94002
(650) 593-9119
www.ppi2pass.com

ISBN: 978-1-59126-179-7

Table of Contents

Preface and Acknowledgments

This book, which is written to help you study for and pass the LEED Green Associate credentialing exam, is a product of my passion for green building. Soon after I began designing mechanical systems, I recognized that many contractors, engineers, product vendors, and architects desired a fundamental understanding of LEED. As a result, I began creating hour-long seminars discussing the impact of buildings on the environment and the growing presence of LEED for the benefit of local building professionals. The success of these local seminars paved the way for me to present LEED exam prep training seminars throughout the country. The problems in this book, which are unique, based on my experiences, and representative of those on the actual exam, are outgrowths of those presentations and seminars.

I wish to acknowledge those who have helped me create this book. First, thanks go to the incredibly talented professionals working at Total Mechanical. Their combined experience across all mechanical trades has proven to be an invaluable resource for me; without their assistance I would not have the broad knowledge of LEED that I have today. Thanks also go to Mike Hyde, Total Mechanical's Chief HVAC Engineer. He continually provides forward thinking solutions to our LEED projects. I am deeply appreciative of the Mechanical Service Contractors of America (MSCA) for hiring me to provide my first LEED exam prep training, and of Barb Dolim, MSCA Executive Director, for providing direction as I developed the training. I would also like to thank all of my LEED seminar attendees, who continually contribute to my understanding and appreciation of the rewards and challenges of green building.

Next, thank you to those at PPI who helped in the process of creating this book, including director of new product development Sarah Hubbard, director of production Cathy Schrott, editorial assistant Courtnee Crystal, and typesetter and cover designer Amy Schwertman.

Finally, I would like to thank my wife, Dana, for her support throughout the entire process.

Despite all of the help and support I had, any mistakes you find are mine. If you find any mistakes, please report them through **www.ppi2pass.com/errata**. Corrections will be posted on the PPI website and incorporated into this book when it is reprinted.

Good luck on the exam and in all your green building efforts.

David M. Hubka, DE, LEED AP

Introduction

About the LEED Credentialing Program

The Green Building Certification Institute (GBCI) offers credentialing opportunities to professionals who demonstrate knowledge of Leadership in Energy and Environmental Design (LEED) green building practices. *LEED GA Practice Exams: Green Associate* prepares you for the LEED Green Associate (GA) exam and part one of each of the LEED Accredited Professional (AP) specialty exams.

GBCI's LEED credentialing program has three tiers. The first tier corresponds to the LEED Green Associate exam. According to the *LEED Green Associate Candidate Handbook*, this exam confirms that you have the knowledge and skills necessary to understand and support green design, construction, and operations. When you pass the LEED Green Associate exam, you will earn the LEED Green Associate credential.

The second tier, which corresponds to the LEED AP specialty exams, confirms your deeper and more specialized knowledge of green building practices. GBCI currently has planned five tracks for the LEED AP exams: LEED AP Homes, LEED AP Operations & Maintenance, LEED AP Building Design & Construction, LEED AP Interior Design & Construction, and LEED AP Neighborhood Development. The LEED AP exams are based on the corresponding LEED reference guide and rating systems and other references. When you pass the LEED Green Associate exam along with any LEED AP specialty exam, you will earn the LEED AP credential.

The third tier, called LEED AP Fellow, will distinguish professionals with an exceptional depth of knowledge, experience, and accomplishments with LEED green building practices. This distinction will be attainable through extensive LEED project experience, not by taking an exam.

For more information about LEED credentialing, visit **www.ppi2pass.com/LEEDhome**.

About the LEED Green Associate Exam

The LEED Green Associate exam contains 100 questions that test your knowledge of green building practices and principles, as well as your familiarity with LEED requirements, resources, and processes. Accordingly, GBCI categorizes the exam questions into the following seven subject areas. GBCI does not indicate how many questions from each subject area will be included in any administration of the exam.

- *Synergistic Opportunities and LEED Application Process* (project requirements; costs; green resources; standards that support LEED credit; credit interactions; Credit Interpretation Requests and rulings; components of LEED online and project registration; components of LEED score card; components of letter templates; strategies to achieve credit; project boundary; LEED boundary; property boundary; prerequisites and/or minimum program requirements for LEED certification; preliminary rating; multiple certifications for same building; occupancy requirements; USGBC policies; requirements to earn LEED AP credit)
- *Project Site Factors* (community connectivity: transportation and pedestrian access; zoning requirements; development: heat islands)
- *Water Management* (types and quality of water; water management)
- *Project Systems and Energy Impacts* (environmental concerns; green power)
- *Acquisition, Installation, and Management of Project Materials* (recycled materials; regionally harvested and manufactured materials; construction waste management)
- *Stakeholder Involvement in Innovation* (integrated project team criteria; durability planning and management; innovative and regional design)
- *Project Surroundings and Public Outreach* (codes)

Taking the LEED Credentialing Exams

To apply for a LEED credentialing exam, you must agree to the disciplinary policy and credential maintenance requirements and submit to an application audit. To be eligible to take the LEED Green Associate exam, one of the following must be true.

- Your line of work is in a sustainable field.
- You have documented experience supporting a LEED-registered project.
- You have attended an education program that addresses green building principles.

To be eligible to take a LEED AP exam, you must have documented experience with a LEED Registered Project within the three years prior to your application submittal.

The LEED credentialing exams are administered by computer at Prometric test sites. Prometric is a third party testing agency with over 250 testing locations in the United States and hundreds of centers globally. To schedule an exam, you must first apply at www.gbci.org to receive an eligibility ID number. Then, you must go to the Prometric website at www.prometric.com/gbci to schedule and pay for the exam. If you need to reschedule or cancel your exam, you must do so directly through Prometric.

The LEED credentialing exam questions are multiple choice with four or more answer options for each question. If more than one option must be selected to correctly answer a question, the question stem will indicate how many options you must choose. Each 100-question exam lasts two hours, giving you a bit more than one and a half minutes per question. The bulk of the questions are non-numerical. Because calculators are not allowed or provided, only basic math is needed to correctly solve any quantitative questions. No reference materials or other supplies may be brought into the exam room, though a pencil and scratch paper will be provided by the testing center. (References are not provided.) The only thing you need to bring with you on exam day is your identification.

Your testing experience begins with an optional brief tutorial to introduce you to the testing computer's functions. When you've finished the tutorial, questions and answer options are shown on a computer screen, and the computer keeps track of which options you choose. Because points are not deducted for incorrectly answered questions, you should mark an answer to every question. For answers you are unsure of, make your best guess and flag the question for later review. If you decide on a different answer later, you can change it, but if you run out of time before getting to all your flagged questions, you still will have given a response to each one. Be sure to mark the correct number of options for each question. There is no partial credit for incomplete answers (or for selecting only some of the correct options).

If you are taking both the first tier (LEED Green Associate) and the second tier (LEED AP) exams on the same day, at the end of your first session the computer will ask you if you are ready to take the second tier. You can take a short break at this time. The second tier's two hours begins when you click "yes" to indicate that you are ready.

To ensure that all candidates' chances of passing remain constant regardless of the difficulty of the specific questions administered on any given exam, GBCI converts the raw exam score to a scaled score, with the total number of points set at 200 and a minimum passing score of 170. In this way, you are not penalized if the exam taken is more difficult than another exam. Instead, in such a case, fewer questions must be answered correctly to achieve a passing score. Your scaled score (or scores, if you are taking both tiers on the same day) is reported on the screen upon completing the exam. A brief optional exit survey completes the exam experience.

When you pass the LEED Green Associate exam, a LEED Green Associate certificate will be sent to you in the mail. If you take and pass both exams, a LEED AP certificate will be sent to you in the mail. If you take both exams but pass only the LEED AP exam, you will need to reregister, retake, and pass the LEED Green Associate exam before you receive any LEED credential.

How to Use This Book

There are a few ways you can use this book's two practice exams. You can do an untimed review of the questions and answers to familiarize yourself with the exam format and content, determine which subjects you are weak in, and use the information as a guide for studying. (Use the materials identified in this book's "References" section as the basis for your exam review.) You can use one or both practice exams to simulate the exam experience either before you begin your study (as a pre-test) or when you think you are fully prepared. Or you can combine these approaches, using one exam to guide your review and the other to simulate the exam experience.

To simulate the exam experience, don't look at the questions or answers ahead of time. Put away your study materials and references, set a timer for two hours, and solve as many questions as you can within the time limit. Practice exam-like time management. Fill in the provided bubble sheet with your best guess on every question regardless of your certainty and mark the answers to revisit if time permits. If you finish before the time is up, review your work. If you are unable to complete the exam within the time limit, make a note of where you were after two hours; but, continue on to complete the exam. Keep track of your time to see how much faster you will need to work to finish the actual exam within two hours.

After taking a practice exam, check your answers against the answer key. Consider a problem correctly answered only if you have selected all of the required options (and no others).

Calculate the percent correct. Though the actual exam score will be scaled, aim for getting at least 70% (70 questions) of the practice exam's questions correct. The fully explained solutions are a learning tool. In addition to reading the solutions to the questions you answered incorrectly, read the explanations to those you answered correctly. Categorize your incorrect responses by exam subject to help you determine the areas you need to study. Use the references list to guide your preparation. Though these exams reflect the breadth and depth of the content on the actual exam, use your best judgment when determining the subjects you need to review.

References

The *LEED GA Practice Exams: Green Associate* is based on the following references, identified by the Green Building Certification Institute (GBCI) in its *LEED Green Associate Candidate Handbook*. All of these references are available electronically. You can find links to these references on PPI's website, **www.ppi2pass.com/LEEDreferences**.

Primary References

Bernheim, Anthony and William Reed. "Part II: Pre-Design Issues." *Sustainable Building Technical Manual*. Public Technology, Inc. 1996.

Cost of Green Revisited: Reexamining the Feasibility and Cost Impact of Sustainable Design in Light of Increased Market Adoption. Sacramento, CA: Davis Langdon, 2007.

Introduction and Glossary. *Existing Buildings: Operations & Maintenance Reference Guide*. Washington, DC: U.S. Green Building Council, 2008.

Guidance on Innovation & Design (ID) Credits. Announcement. Washington, DC: U.S. Green Building Council, 2004.

Guidelines for CIR Customers. Announcement. Washington, DC: U.S. Green Building Council, 2007.

LEED for Homes Rating System. Washington, DC: U.S.Green Building Council, 2008.

LEED Technical and Scientific Advisory Committee. *The Treatment by LEED of the Environmental Impact of HVAC Refrigerants*. Washington, DC: U.S. Green Building Council, 2004.

Secondary References

AIA Integrated Project Delivery: A Guide. American Institute of Architects, 2007.

Americans with Disabilities Act: Standards for Accessible Design. 28 CFR Part 36. Washington, DC: Code of Federal Regulations, 1994.

"Codes and Standards." Washington, DC: International Code Council, 2009.

"Construction and Building Inspectors." *Occupational Outlook Handbook*. Washington, DC: Bureau of Labor Statistics, 2009.

Frankel, Mark and Cathy Turner. *Energy Performance of LEED for New Construction Buildings: Final Report*. Vancouver, WA: New Buildings Institute and U.S. Green Building Council, 2008.

GSA 2003 Facilities Standards. Washington, DC: General Services Administration, 2003.

Guide to Purchasing Green Power: Renewable Electricity, Renewable Energy Certifications, and On-Site Renewable Generation. Washington, DC: Environmental Protection Agency, 2004.

Kareis, Brian. *Review of ANSI/ASHRAE Standard 62.1-2004: Ventilation for Acceptable Indoor Air Quality*. Greensboro, NC: Workplace Group, 2007.

Lee, Kun-Mo and Haruo Uehara. *Best Practices of ISO - 14021: Self-Declared Environmental Claims*. Suwon, Korea: Ajou University, 2003.

LEED Steering Committee. *Foundations of the Leadership in Energy and Environmental Design Rating System: A Tool for Market Transformation*. Washington, DC: U.S. Green Building Council, 2006.

Practice Exam One

1. (A) (B) (C) (D)
2. (A) (B) (C) (D) (E)
3. (A) (B) (C) (D)
4. (A) (B) (C) (D) (E)
5. (A) (B) (C) (D) (E)
6. (A) (B) (C) (D) (E)
7. (A) (B) (C) (D) (E)
8. (A) (B) (C) (D) (E)
9. (A) (B) (C) (D) (E)
10. (A) (B) (C) (D) (E)
11. (A) (B) (C) (D)
12. (A) (B) (C) (D)
13. (A) (B) (C) (D)
14. (A) (B) (C) (D) (E)
15. (A) (B) (C) (D) (E)
16. (A) (B) (C) (D) (E)
17. (A) (B) (C) (D)
18. (A) (B) (C) (D)
19. (A) (B) (C) (D)
20. (A) (B) (C) (D) (E)
21. (A) (B) (C) (D) (E)
22. (A) (B) (C) (D) (E)
23. (A) (B) (C) (D) (E)
24. (A) (B) (C) (D)
25. (A) (B) (C) (D) (E)

26. (A) (B) (C) (D) (E)
27. (A) (B) (C) (D)
28. (A) (B) (C) (D) (E)
29. (A) (B) (C) (D)
30. (A) (B) (C) (D)
31. (A) (B) (C) (D) (E)
32. (A) (B) (C) (D)
33. (A) (B) (C) (D)
34. (A) (B) (C) (D) (E)
35. (A) (B) (C) (D)
36. (A) (B) (C) (D) (E) (F)
37. (A) (B) (C) (D)
38. (A) (B) (C) (D) (E)
39. (A) (B) (C) (D)
40. (A) (B) (C) (D) (E)
41. (A) (B) (C) (D)
42. (A) (B) (C) (D) (E) (F)
43. (A) (B) (C) (D) (E)
44. (A) (B) (C) (D) (E)
45. (A) (B) (C) (D)
46. (A) (B) (C) (D)
47. (A) (B) (C) (D)
48. (A) (B) (C) (D) (E)
49. (A) (B) (C) (D)
50. (A) (B) (C) (D)

51. (A) (B) (C) (D) (E)
52. (A) (B) (C) (D) (E) (F)
53. (A) (B) (C) (D)
54. (A) (B) (C) (D) (E)
55. (A) (B) (C) (D) (E)
56. (A) (B) (C) (D) (E)
57. (A) (B) (C) (D) (E) (F) (G)
58. (A) (B) (C) (D) (E)
59. (A) (B) (C) (D)
60. (A) (B) (C) (D) (E)
61. (A) (B) (C) (D) (E)
62. (A) (B) (C) (D)
63. (A) (B) (C) (D) (E)
64. (A) (B) (C) (D)
65. (A) (B) (C) (D)
66. (A) (B) (C) (D) (E) (F)
67. (A) (B) (C) (D) (E)
68. (A) (B) (C) (D)
69. (A) (B) (C) (D)
70. (A) (B) (C) (D)
71. (A) (B) (C) (D) (E)
72. (A) (B) (C) (D)
73. (A) (B) (C) (D)
74. (A) (B) (C) (D)
75. (A) (B) (C) (D)

76. Ⓐ Ⓑ Ⓒ Ⓓ Ⓔ
77. Ⓐ Ⓑ Ⓒ Ⓓ Ⓔ
78. Ⓐ Ⓑ Ⓒ Ⓓ
79. Ⓐ Ⓑ Ⓒ Ⓓ
80. Ⓐ Ⓑ Ⓒ Ⓓ
81. Ⓐ Ⓑ Ⓒ Ⓓ Ⓔ
82. Ⓐ Ⓑ Ⓒ Ⓓ
83. Ⓐ Ⓑ Ⓒ Ⓓ
84. Ⓐ Ⓑ Ⓒ Ⓓ Ⓔ Ⓕ
85. Ⓐ Ⓑ Ⓒ Ⓓ
86. Ⓐ Ⓑ Ⓒ Ⓓ Ⓔ Ⓕ
87. Ⓐ Ⓑ Ⓒ Ⓓ
88. Ⓐ Ⓑ Ⓒ Ⓓ Ⓔ
89. Ⓐ Ⓑ Ⓒ Ⓓ Ⓔ

90. Ⓐ Ⓑ Ⓒ Ⓓ Ⓔ
91. Ⓐ Ⓑ Ⓒ Ⓓ
92. Ⓐ Ⓑ Ⓒ Ⓓ Ⓔ
93. Ⓐ Ⓑ Ⓒ Ⓓ Ⓔ
94. Ⓐ Ⓑ Ⓒ Ⓓ
95. Ⓐ Ⓑ Ⓒ Ⓓ
96. Ⓐ Ⓑ Ⓒ Ⓓ Ⓔ Ⓕ Ⓖ
97. Ⓐ Ⓑ Ⓒ Ⓓ Ⓔ
98. Ⓐ Ⓑ Ⓒ Ⓓ
99. Ⓐ Ⓑ Ⓒ Ⓓ Ⓔ
100. Ⓐ Ⓑ Ⓒ Ⓓ

1. Who can view CIRs posted to the USGBC website? (Choose two.)

   (A) individuals with a USGBC website account
   (B) registered employees of USGBC member companies
   (C) LEED Accredited Professionals
   (D) registered project team members

2. LEED project teams can earn an "extra" point by achieving _____ performance. (Choose two.)

   (A) exemplary
   (B) ideal
   (C) innovative
   (D) original
   (E) perfect

3. Potable water can also be called _____.

   (A) drinking water
   (B) graywater
   (C) blackwater
   (D) rainwater

4. To increase a LEED project's chances of success, team members should be involved with which of the following project phases? (Choose three.)

   (A) concept
   (B) design development
   (C) inspector site visits
   (D) ongoing commissioning
   (E) construction

5. LEED generally groups credits by credit categories, but the LEED O&M reference guide introduction describes an alternative way of grouping the credits: by their functional characteristics. Which of the following are identified as functional characteristic groups? (Choose two.)

   (A) Administration
   (B) Materials In
   (C) Sustainable Sites
   (D) Waste Management
   (E) Water Efficiency

6. A LEED project is more likely to stay within budget when the team does which of the following? (Choose three.)

   (A) submits documentation for as few LEED credits as possible
   (B) adheres to the plan throughout project
   (C) aligns goals with budget
   (D) contacts USGBC for budget guidance
   (E) establishes project goals and expectations

7. Projects located in urban areas can utilize which of the following to meet LEED open space requirements? (Choose two.)

   (A) accessible roof decks
   (B) landscaping with indigenous plants
   (C) non-vehicular, pedestrian orientated hardscapes
   (D) onsite photovoltaics
   (E) pervious parking lots

8. Which of the following can affect a building's energy efficiency? (Choose three.)

   (A) building orientation
   (B) envelope thermal efficiency
   (C) HVAC system sizing
   (D) refrigerant selection
   (E) VOC content of building materials

9. Which of the following are included in calculations used to determine life-cycle costs? (Choose two.)

   (A) equipment
   (B) facility alterations
   (C) maintenance
   (D) occupant transportation
   (E) utilities

10. Which of the following are NOT common benefits of daylighting? (Choose two.)

    (A) increased productivity
    (B) reduced air pollution
    (C) reduced heat island effect
    (D) reduced light pollution
    (E) reduced operating costs

11. The LEED CI rating system can be applied to which of the following projects? (Choose two.)

    (A) major envelope renovation of a building

    (B) renovation of part of an owner-occupied building

    (C) tenant infill of an existing building

    (D) upgrades to the operation and maintenance of an existing facility

12. Certain prerequisites and credits require project teams to create policies. What information should be included in a policy model? (Choose two.)

    (A) performance period

    (B) policy author

    (C) responsible party

    (D) time period

13. The primary function of which of the following is to encourage sustainable building design, construction, and operation?

    (A) chain-of-custody

    (B) the LEED rating systems

    (C) standard operating procedures (SOPs)

    (D) waste reduction program

14. What information is required to register a project for LEED certification? (Choose three.)

    (A) list of LEED project team members

    (B) name of LEED AP who will be working on project

    (C) primary contact information

    (D) project owner information

    (E) project type

15. Which of the following are among the five basic steps for pursing LEED for Homes certification? (Choose two.)

    (A) achieve certification as a LEED home

    (B) become a USGBC member company

    (C) create list of LEED certified products to be used

    (D) include appliances only if they are Energy Star-rated

    (E) market and sell the home

16. Fire suppression systems that use which of the following will contribute the least to ozone depletion? (Choose two.)

   (A) chloroflourocarbons
   (B) halons
   (C) hydrochlorofluorocarbons
   (D) hydrofluorocarbons
   (E) water

17. Which of the following describes the *property area*?

   (A) area of the project site impacted by the building and hardscapes
   (B) area of the project site impacted by hardscapes only
   (C) area of the project site impacted by the building only
   (D) total area of the site including constructed and non-constructed areas

18. Which LEED rating system includes performance periods and requires recertification to maintain the building's LEED certification?

   (A) LEED CI
   (B) LEED CS
   (C) LEED EBO&M
   (D) LEED NC

19. For a credit uploaded to LEED Online, a white check mark next to a credit name indicates that the credit is _____.

   (A) being pursued and no online documentation has been uploaded
   (B) being pursued and some online documentation has been uploaded
   (C) complete and ready for submission
   (D) not being pursued

20. Remodeling an older existing building may help a project team achieve credit for building reuse and prevent a project team from achieving credit for _____. (Choose three.)

   (A) controllability of systems
   (B) energy use reduction
   (C) regional materials
   (D) sustainable site use
   (E) water use reduction

21. LEED CS (rather than LEED NC) should be pursued when which of the following items are outside the control of the building owner? (Choose three.)

    (A) envelope insulation

    (B) interior finishes

    (C) lighting

    (D) mechanical distribution

    (E) site selection

22. LEED Online provides a means for _____. (Choose two.)

    (A) code officials to access project documentation

    (B) product vendors to advertize

    (C) project team members to analyze anticipated building energy performance

    (D) project administrators to manage LEED projects

    (E) project team members to manage LEED prerequisites and credits

23. Installing a green roof can help a project team achieve which of the following LEED credits? (Choose two.)

    (A) Development Density and Community Connectivity

    (B) Heat Island Effect

    (C) Light Pollution Reduction

    (D) Site Selection

    (E) Stormwater Design

24. Using light bulbs with low mercury content, long life, and high lumen output will result in which of the following?

    (A) improved indoor air quality

    (B) increased light pollution

    (C) reduced light pollution

    (D) reduced toxic waste

25. Which of the following are covered in the Sustainable Sites credit category? (Choose three.)

    (A) light to night sky

    (B) light trespass

    (C) on-site renewable energy

    (D) stormwater mitigation

    (E) refrigerants

26. Which of the following tasks must be part of a durability plan? (Choose two.)

    (A) assign responsibilities for plan implementation

    (B) evaluate durability risks of project

    (C) incorporate durability strategies into design

    (D) research local codes

    (E) submit CIR for available list of durability strategies

27. What is the role of the TSAC? (Choose two.)

    (A) ensure the technical soundness of the LEED reference guides and training

    (B) maintain technical rigor and consistency in the development of LEED credits

    (C) resolve issues to maintain consistency across different LEED rating systems

    (D) respond to CIRs submitted by LEED project teams

28. Project teams can earn credit for purchasing sustainable ongoing consumables within the LEED EBO&M rating system. Ongoing consumables containing a defined amount of _____ are considered sustainable. (Choose three.)

    (A) material certified by the Rainforest Alliance

    (B) preindustrial material

    (C) rapidly renewable material

    (D) regionally extracted material

    (E) salvaged material

29. Within an existing building undergoing major renovations, a tenant is pursuing LEED certification. Which rating system should the tenant use to earn a LEED plaque?

    (A) LEED CI

    (B) LEED CS

    (C) LEED EBO&M

    (D) LEED NC

30. Regional Priority credits vary depending on a project's _____.

    (A) certification level

    (B) community connectivity

    (C) development density

    (D) geographic location

31. Which of the following costs should be considered prior to pursuing a LEED credit? (Choose three.)

    (A) application review cost

    (B) construction cost

    (C) documentation cost

    (D) registration cost

    (E) soft cost

32. Which rating system include CIRs, appeals, and performance periods?

    (A) LEED CI
    (B) LEED CS
    (C) LEED EBO&M
    (D) LEED NC

33. Which standard addresses energy-efficient building design?

    (A) ASHRAE 55-2004
    (B) ANSI/ASHRAE 52.2-1999
    (C) ANSI/ASHRAE 62.1-2007
    (D) ANSI/ASHRAE/IESNA 90.1-2007

34. Which of the following credits will NOT be directly affected by a project team intending to increase a building's ventilation? (Choose two.)

    (A) Controllability of Systems
    (B) Enhanced Commissioning
    (C) Indoor Chemical and Pollutant Source Control
    (D) Measurement and Verification
    (E) Optimize Energy Performance

35. Which of the following describes the purpose of a chain-of-custody document?

    (A) track the movement of products from extraction to the production site
    (B) track the movement of wood products from the forest to the building site
    (C) verify rapidly renewable materials
    (D) verify recycled content

36. A material must be which of the following for it to qualify as a *regional material* within the LEED rating systems? (Choose two.)

    (A) FSC-certified
    (B) made from 10% post-consumer content
    (C) made from products that take 10 years or less to grow
    (D) manufactured within 500 miles of the project site
    (E) permanently installed on the project site
    (F) used to create process equipment

37. A project team's choice of paint will NOT affect which of the following credits?

    (A) Heat Island Effect
    (B) Low-Emitting Materials
    (C) Materials Reuse
    (D) Rapidly Renewable Materials

38. Which of the following do all LEED rating systems contain? (Choose three.)

     (A) core credits
     (B) educational credits
     (C) innovation credits
     (D) operational credits
     (E) prerequisites

39. Which of the following is NOT an example of a durable good?

     (A) computer
     (B) door
     (C) landscaping equipment
     (D) office desk

40. Which of the following would most likely be affected by an increase in ventilation? (Choose two.)

     (A) construction costs
     (B) interior temperature set points
     (C) local climate
     (D) operational costs
     (E) refrigerant management

41. Which items should be considered when selecting refrigerants for a building's HVAC & R system? (Choose two.)

     (A) global depletion potential
     (B) global warming potential
     (C) ozone depletion potential
     (D) ozone warming potential

42. Which information is required to set up a personal account on the USGBC website? (Choose three.)

     (A) company name
     (B) email address
     (C) industry sector
     (D) LEED credentialing exam date
     (E) phone number
     (F) prior LEED projects worked on

43. Project teams must comply with which of the following CIRs? (Choose two.)

    (A) CIRs appealed prior to project registration, for all rating systems

    (B) CIRs reviewed by a TAG for their own project

    (C) CIRs reviewed by a TAG prior to project registration, for projects within the project's climate region

    (D) CIRs posted prior to project application, for the applicable rating system only

    (E) CIRs posted prior to project completion, for projects within their own project's climate region

44. Which of the following describe methods of earning exemplary performance credit? (Choose two.)

    (A) achieve 75% of the credits in each LEED category

    (B) achieve every LEED credit in the Energy and Atmosphere category

    (C) achieve the next incremental level of an existing credit

    (D) double the requirements of an existing credit

    (E) pursue LEED CI certification within a LEED CS-certified building

45. Which of the following potable water conserving strategies may help a project team achieve a LEED point? (Choose two.)

    (A) collecting blackwater for landscape irrigation

    (B) collecting rainwater for sewage conveyance

    (C) installing an on-site septic tank

    (D) using cooling condensate for cooling tower make-up

46. Which of the following requires an explanation of the proposed credit requirements?

    (A) CIR submittal

    (B) Innovation in Design exemplary performance submittal

    (C) LEED credit equivalence submittal

    (D) LEED Online letter template submittal

47. Which of the following organizations defines the off-site renewable energy sources eligible for LEED credits?

    (A) Center for Research and Development of Green Power

    (B) Center for Resource Solutions

    (C) Department of Energy

    (D) Energy Star

48. The International Code Council (ICC) includes which of the following codes? (Choose three.)

    (A) International Building Automation Code (IBAC)

    (B) International Energy Conservation Code (IECC)

    (C) International Lighting Code (ILC)

    (D) International Mechanical Code (IMC)

    (E) International Plumbing Code (IPC)

49. Which of the following is true?

    (A) A LEED project administrator must be a LEED AP.

    (B) Buildings can be LEED-accredited.

    (C) Companies can be USGBC members.

    (D) People can be LEED-certified.

50. In addition to satisfying all prerequisites, what is the minimum percentage of points that a project team can earn to achieve LEED Platinum certification?

    (A) 70%

    (B) 80%

    (C) 90%

    (D) 100%

51. LEED submittal templates provide which of the following? (Choose two.)

    (A) a list of potential strategies to achieve a credit or prerequisite

    (B) a means to modify project documentation

    (C) a means to submit a project for review

    (D) a means to review and submit CIRs

    (E) the project's final scorecard

52. According to the *Sustainable Building Technical Manual*, which of the following are key steps of an environmentally responsive design process? (Choose three.)

    (A) bid

    (B) design

    (C) post-design

    (D) pre-design

    (E) re-bid

    (F) vendor selection

53. Which is true of the LEED CI rating system?

    (A) Precertification allows the owner to market to potential tenants.

    (B) Projects can earn a point for prohibiting smoking within the tenant space.

    (C) Projects can earn half points under the Site Selection credit.

    (D) Projects must recertify every five years to maintain certification status.

54. Once a project undergoes a construction review, what are the potential rulings for each submitted prerequisite and credit? (Choose three.)

    (A) anticipated

    (B) clarify

    (C) deferred

    (D) denied

    (E) earned

55. What is the role of the LEED Steering Committee? (Choose two.)

    (A) delegate responsibility and oversee all LEED committee activities

    (B) develop LEED accreditation exams

    (C) ensure that LEED and its supporting documentation is technically sound

    (D) establish and enforce LEED direction and policy

    (E) respond to CIRs submitted by LEED project teams

56. The LEED Online workspace allows the LEED project administrator to do which of the following? (Choose three.)

    (A) apply for LEED EBO&M precertification

    (B) assign credits to project team members

    (C) build a project team

    (D) review credit appeals submitted by other project teams

    (E) submit projects for review

57. Which of the following items are free? (Choose three.)

    (A) a project's first CIR

    (B) LEED BD & C reference guide

    (C) LEED brochure

    (D) LEED certification

    (E) LEED for Homes rating system

    (F) sample LEED submittal templates

    (G) usgbc.org account

58. What happens if a CIR extends beyond the expertise of the assigned TAG? (Choose two.)

    (A) additional response time may be incurred

    (B) it is rejected

    (C) it is sent to the LEED Steering Committee

    (D) it must be submitted as an Innovation in Design credit

    (E) the TAG will provide the ruling

59. What becomes available once a project is registered?

    (A) LEED project tools

    (B) posted CIRs

    (C) posted credit appeals

    (D) sample submittal templates

60. The LEED rating systems require compliance with which of the following? (Choose two.)

    (A) codes and regulations that address asbestos and water discharge

    (B) codes and regulations that address PCBs and water management

    (C) referenced standards that address fixture performance requirements for water use

    (D) referenced standards that address sustainable forest management practices

    (E) referenced standards that address VOCs

61. Which of the following steps are part of creating an integrated project team? (Choose two.)

    (A) include members from varying industry sectors

    (B) include product vendors in the design phase

    (C) involve a commissioning authority in team members' selection

    (D) involve the LEED AP in design integration

    (E) involve the team in different project phases

62. Facilities undergoing minor alterations and system upgrades must follow which rating system?

    (A) LEED CI

    (B) LEED CS

    (C) LEED EBO&M

    (D) LEED NC

63. Which of the following strategies may help a project team achieve a LEED credit? (Choose two.)

(A) establish an erosion and sedimentation plan

(B) establish a location for the storage and collection of recyclables

(C) install HCFC-based HVAC & R equipment

(D) use rainwater for sewage conveyance or landscape irrigation

(E) remediate contaminated soil

64. Which of the following statements is true?

(A) CIRs are reviewed by a TAG at no additional charge once a project is registered.

(B) The first step toward LEED certification is passing the Green Associate exam.

(C) The LEED rating system only applies to commercial buildings.

(D) To achieve LEED certification, every prerequisite and a minimum number of credits must be achieved.

65. Installing ground source heat pumps would help a project team achieve which of the following credits or prerequisites?

(A) Green Power

(B) Optimize Energy Performance

(C) On-Site Renewable Energy

(D) Water Use Reduction

66. What are the goals of the Portfolio Program? (Choose two.)

(A) create a volume accreditation path

(B) encourage global adoption of sustainable green building practices

(C) exceed the requirements of ANSI/ASHRAE/IESNA 90.1-2007 by a rating system-designated percentage

(D) offer a volume certification path

(E) provide a streamlined certification process for large-scale projects

(F) provide a template of key data for the design team members to compile

67. When should a LEED project's budget be addressed? (Choose two.)

(A) before the design phase

(B) during the construction phase

(C) during the selection of construction team

(D) during the selection of design team

(E) upon project completion

68. Which of the following could help minimize potable water used for the site landscaping and contribute toward earning a LEED landscaping credit?

    (A) designing the site, or the building's roof, with no landscaping

    (B) installing invasive plants

    (C) installing native or adapted plants

    (D) installing turf grass

69. How many Regional Priority points are available for LEED projects?

    (A) 2 points

    (B) 4 points

    (C) 6 points

    (D) 8 points

70. A project team chooses to group credits by functional characteristics. Credits focusing on the measurement of a building's energy performance and ozone protection would be grouped into which of the following categories?

    (A) Energy and Atmosphere

    (B) Energy Metrics

    (C) Materials Out

    (D) Site Management

71. Which of the following are considered principle durability risks? (Choose three.)

    (A) heat islands

    (B) interior moisture loads

    (C) ozone depletion

    (D) pests

    (E) ultraviolet radiation

72. What is the first step of the LEED for Homes certification process?

    (A) become a LEED AP

    (B) contact a LEED for Homes provider

    (C) register with GBCI

    (D) submit a CIR

73. HVAC & R equipment with _____ will contribute to ozone depletion and global warming.

    (A) a manufacture date prior to 2005

    (B) a relatively long equipment life

    (C) minimal refrigerant charge

    (D) refrigerant leakage

74. Sealing ventilation ducts, installing rodent and corrosion proof screens, and using air sealing pump covers are strategies that could be a part of which of the following?

  (A) design charrette

  (B) durability plan

  (C) landscape management plan

  (D) PE exemption form

75. Which standard addresses thermal comfort of building occupants?

  (A) ASHRAE 55-2004

  (B) ANSI/ASHRAE 52.2-1999

  (C) ANSI/ASHRAE 62.1-2007

  (D) ANSI/ASHRAE/IESNA 90.1-2007

76. A LEED project's primary contact must submit which of the following when registering a project? (Choose three.)

  (A) email address

  (B) LEED AP certificate

  (C) LEED project history

  (D) organization name

  (E) individual's title

77. Prior to registering a LEED project, which of the following must be confirmed? (Choose two.)

  (A) necessary CIRs

  (B) precertification

  (C) project cost

  (D) project summary

  (E) project team members

78. Water lost through plant transpiration and evaporation from soil is described by the term _____.

  (A) evapotranspiration

  (B) infiltration

  (C) sublimation

  (D) surface runoff

79. Individuals with a LEED reference guide electronic access code can do which of the following?

  (A) join a LEED project as a team member

  (B) print the LEED reference guide

  (C) purchase a LEED reference guide

  (D) view a protected electronic version of the LEED reference guide

80. LEED credits and prerequisites are presented in a common format in all versions of LEED rating systems. The structure includes which of the following?

    (A) economic impact

    (B) greening opportunities

    (C) intent

    (D) submittal requirements

81. The Materials and Resources category directly addresses which of the following? (Choose two.)

    (A) habitat conservation

    (B) durable goods

    (C) energy consumption

    (D) landscape

    (E) waste stream

82. Building on which of the following sites will most likely have the smallest impact on the environment?

    (A) greenfield

    (B) public parklands

    (C) previously undeveloped site

    (D) urban area

83. LEED submittal templates require which of the following items? (Choose two.)

    (A) declarant's name

    (B) product manufacturer

    (C) project area

    (D) project location

84. The pre-design phase of a LEED project should include which of the following steps? (Choose three.)

    (A) commissioning mechanical systems

    (B) establishing a project budget

    (C) establishing project goals

    (D) site selection

    (E) testing and balancing mechanical systems

    (F) training maintenance staff

85. Which is true about a CIR submittal?

    (A) CIRs must be submitted as text-based inquiries.

    (B) Drawings and specification sheets must be submitted as attachments.

    (C) It must include a complete project narrative.

    (D) Text is limited to 1000 words.

86. Green building design and construction decisions should be guided by which of the following items? (Choose three.)

    (A) bid cost
    (B) construction documents
    (C) design cost
    (D) energy efficiency
    (E) environmental impact
    (F) indoor environment

87. GBCI is a non-profit organization that provides which of the following services? (Choose two.)

    (A) accreditation of industry professionals
    (B) certification of sustainable products
    (C) certification of sustainable buildings
    (D) educational programs on sustainability topics

88. Credits can be earned after which of the following project phases? (Choose two.)

    (A) appeal
    (B) design
    (C) certification
    (D) construction
    (E) post-construction

89. What are the short-term benefits of commissioning? (Choose two.)

    (A) assures credit achievement
    (B) decreases initial project cost
    (C) promotes code compliance
    (D) promotes design efficiency
    (E) reduces design and construction time

90. Conventional fossil-based electricity generation results in which of the following emissions? (Choose three.)

    (A) anthropogenic nitrogen oxide
    (B) carbon dioxide
    (C) carbon monoxide
    (D) sulfur dioxide
    (E) VOCs

91. Which strategy helps minimize a site's heat island effect?

    (A) having a high glazing factor

    (B) installing hardscapes with low SRI values

    (C) maximizing the area of site hardscapes

    (D) shading hardscapes with vegetation

92. The BOD, which includes design information necessary to accomplish the owner's project requirements, must contain which of the following? (Choose three.)

    (A) building materials selection

    (B) indoor environmental quality criteria

    (C) mechanical systems descriptions

    (D) process equipment energy consumption information

    (E) references to applicable codes

93. An integrated project team should include which of the following professionals? (Choose two.)

    (A) code official

    (B) energy sustainability consultant

    (C) landscape architect

    (D) product manufacturer

    (E) utility manager

94. A project is considered a major renovation when at least _____ of the building envelope, interior, or mechanical systems is modified.

    (A) 50%

    (B) 60%

    (C) 70%

    (D) 80%

95. A building that will be partially occupied by the owner may pursue LEED CS certification if the building owner occupies no more than _____ of the building's leasable space.

    (A) 25%

    (B) 50%

    (C) 75%

    (D) 80%

96. The LEED EBO&M rating system includes a Best Management Practices prerequisite. This prerequisite would most likely fall under which of the following credit groupings? (Choose two.)

    (A) Energy and Atmosphere
    (B) Indoor Environmental Quality
    (C) Innovation in Design
    (D) Materials and Resources
    (E) Occupant Health and Productivity
    (F) Operational Effectiveness
    (G) Site Management

97. The Project Details section of the LEED project registration form requires which of the following? (Choose three.)

    (A) company names of all team members
    (B) gross area of the building
    (C) list of likely innovation credits to be pursued
    (D) project budget
    (E) site conditions

98. To be eligible for LEED recertification, a project must be

    (A) precertified under the LEED for Homes rating system
    (B) previously certified under the LEED EBO&M rating system
    (C) previously certified as LEED Platinum under the LEED CS rating system
    (D) previously certified at any level other than LEED Platinum under the LEED NC rating system

99. Which of the following can help reduce a building's energy load? (Choose two.)

    (A) reducing the building's heat island effect
    (B) increasing the ventilation rate
    (C) installing heat recovery systems
    (D) flushing out prior to occupancy
    (E) zoning mechanical systems

100. Minimizing which of the following will improve a building's indoor environmental quality?

    (A) acoustical control
    (B) natural lighting
    (C) ventilation rates
    (D) VOC content in building materials

Practice Exam One Solutions

1. B, D
2. A, C
3. A
4. A, B, E
5. A, B
6. B, C
7. A
8. A, B, C
9. C
10. C, D
11. B, C
12. C, D
13. B
14. C, D
15. A
16. D, E
17. D
18. C
19. B
20. B, C, D
21. B, C, D
22. B, C, D
23. A
24. D
25. A, B, E

26. B, C
27. A, C, D
28. B, C, D
29. A
30. D
31. B, C, E
32. C
33. D
34. C
35. B
36. D, E, F
37. C
38. A, C, D
39. B
40. C, D
41. B, C
42. B, C, E, F
43. B, D
44. C, D
45. B
46. C
47. B
48. B, D
49. C
50. B

51. C, E
52. A, B, D
53. C
54. B, D
55. D
56. B, C
57. E, F, G
58. A, C
59. A
60. B
61. D
62. C
63. D
64. D
65. B
66. D, E
67. A, B
68. C
69. B
70. B
71. B, D
72. B
73. D
74. B
75. A

76. ● (B) (C) ● ●
77. (A) (B) (C) ● ●
78. ● (B) (C) (D)
79. (A) (B) (C) ●
80. (A) (B) ● (D)
81. (A) ● (C) (D) ●
82. (A) (B) (C) ●
83. ● (B) (C) (D)
84. (A) ● ● ● (E) (F)
85. ● (B) (C) (D)
86. (A) (B) (C) ● ● ●
87. ● (B) ● (D)
88. ● (B) (C) ● (E)
89. (A) (B) (C) ● ●

90. ● ● (C) ● (E)
91. (A) (B) (C) ●
92. (A) ● ● (D) ●
93. (A) ● ● (D) (E)
94. ● (B) (C) (D)
95. (A) ● (C) (D)
96. ● (B) (C) (D) (E) ● (G)
97. (A) ● (C) ● ●
98. (A) ● (C) (D)
99. (A) (B) ● (D) ●
100. (A) (B) (C) ●

1. *The answers are:* (B) registered employees of USGBC member companies
    (D) registered project team members

Only members of a LEED project team and employees of a USGBC member company may view posted CIRs.

2. *The answers are:* (A) exemplary
    (C) innovative

To earn points in the Innovation in Design category, project teams can exceed the requirements of an existing LEED credit and earn exemplary performance points, or they can implement innovative performance strategies not addressed by the LEED rating systems.

3. *The answer is:* (A) drinking water

Potable water is water that meets or exceeds EPA drinking water standards and is supplied from wells or municipal water systems.

4. *The answers are:* (A) concept
    (B) design development
    (E) construction

LEED projects benefit from the inclusion of project team members in ongoing commissioning and inspector site visits; however, team member participation is most valuable during the design and construction phases of the project.

5. *The answers are:* (A) Administration
    (B) Materials In

The functional characteristic groups established under the EBO&M rating system are Materials In (includes credits addressing the sustainable purchasing policy of a building), Materials Out, Administration (includes credits addressing the planning and logistics support of operating a high-performance building), Green Cleaning, Site Management, Occupational Health and Productivity, Energy Metrics, and Operational Effectiveness. Sustainable Sites and Water Efficiency are credit categories, not functional characteristic groups. Waste Management is neither a credit category nor a functional characteristic group.

6. *The answers are:* (B) adheres to the plan throughout project
    (C) aligns goals with budget
    (E) establishes project goals and expectations

A project is more likely to stay within budget when the goals and budget are coordinated and when the project team adheres to the plan and frequently checks expenses against the budget. USGBC does not provide guidance for project budgeting. Submitting documentation for fewer credits does not necessarily lead to a successful LEED project budget.

7. *The answers are:* (A) accessible roof decks
    (C) non-vehicular, pedestrian orientated hardscapes

Projects located in urban areas (those buildings with little or no setback) can utilize pedestrian hardscapes, pocket parks, accessible roof decks, plazas, and courtyards to meet the open space requirements.

On-site photovoltaics contribute to on-site renewable energy generation. Pervious parking lots contribute to on-site stormwater mitigation. Landscaping with indigenous plants may reduce the amount of water needed for irrigation. None of these strategies contribute to open space requirements.

8. **The answers are:** (A) building orientation

(B) envelope thermal efficiency

(C) HVAC system sizing

A building's overall energy consumption can vary depending on building orientation, building location, envelope insulation, fenestration u-values, the size of the HVAC system, and electricity requirements of lighting and appliances. Addressing these factors during the design can result in reduced energy bills for the life of the building. Refrigerant selection affects the building's environmental impact (but not the HVAC system efficiency), and volatile organic compound (VOC) content affects indoor air quality.

9. **The answers are:** (C) maintenance

(E) utilities

Life-cycle costing is an accounting methodology used to evaluate the economic performance of a product or system over its useful life. Life-cycle cost calculations include maintenance and operating costs (including the cost of utilities). Neither the occupants' individual expenses nor the initial cost of an investment factor into a building's life-cycle costs.

10. **The answers are:** (C) reduced heat island effect

(D) reduced light pollution

The primary purpose of increasing a building's daylighting is to reduce the need for electric light. Reducing electric light use results in reduced electricity use in general, thereby reducing energy costs and the carbon dioxide emissions (or air pollution) created by the building. Additionally, statistics show that productivity is markedly improved in day lit buildings compared to buildings that rely heavily on electric lighting.

Light pollution is related to the amount of light transmitted from a building afterhours. Daylighting is related to daytime lighting of the interior of the building. A building's heat islands are not affected by daylighting.

11. **The answers are:** (B) renovation of part of an owner-occupied building

(C) tenant infill of an existing building

The LEED for Commercial Interiors (CI) rating system provides the opportunity for tenant spaces and parts of buildings to achieve LEED certification. Major building envelope renovations would be certified under the LEED for New Construction (NC) rating system. Upgrades to the operations and maintenance of an existing facility would be certified under the LEED for Existing Buildings: Operations & Maintenance (EBO&M) rating system.

12. *The answers are:* (C) responsible party

(D) time period

Each policy should identify the individual or team responsible its implementation. Additionally, the time period over which the policy is applicable should be indentified. The time period is not necessarily the same amount of time as the performance period. Note that performance periods only apply to LEED EBO&M projects.

13. *The answer is:* (B) the LEED rating systems

Chain-of-custody is a procedure to document the status of a product from the point-of-harvest or extraction to the ultimate consumer end use and can promote sustainable construction. Standard operating procedures (SOPs) are detailed, written instructions that document a method with the intention of achieving uniformity. A waste reduction program helps a project team minimize waste by using source reduction, reuse, and recycling. Both SOPs and waste reduction programs promote sustainable operations. Of the answer options, only the LEED rating systems support design, construction, and operations.

14. *The answers are:* (C) primary contact information

(D) project owner information

(E) project type

To register a project for LEED certification, the registrant must provide account login information, primary contact information, project owner information, general project information, payment information, and the project type. Project team member names do not have to be submitted to complete the registration form. LEED projects are not required to have a LEED AP on the team.

15. *The answers are:* (A) achieve certification as a LEED home

(E) market and sell the home

The five basic steps of the LEED for Homes are

1. contact a LEED for Homes Certification provider and join the program

2. identify the project team

3. build the home to the stated goals

4. achieve certification as a LEED home

5. market and sell the home

Becoming a USGBC member company reduces the registration fee; however, it is not a basic step.

16. *The answers are:* (D) hydrofluorocarbons

(E) water

Using halons, chlorofluorocarbons, and hydrochlorofluorocarbons in fire suppression systems can lead to ozone depletion. Using water and hydroflourocarbons will have a minimal effect on ozone depletion.

17. *The answer is:* (D) total area of the site including constructed and non-constructed areas

The total area within the legal property boundaries of the site is considered the property area. The project site area that includes constructed and non-constructed areas is defined as the development footprint.

18. *The answer is:* (C) LEED EBO&M

LEED EBO&M is the only rating system that includes performance periods and a recertification requirement. LEED EBO&M projects may recertify as often as every year, and must recertify at least every five years to maintain their LEED certification status.

19. *The answer is:* (B) being pursued and some online documentation has been uploaded

A white check mark indicates that the credit is being pursued and has been assigned to a project member. Some documentation has been uploaded; however, additional info needs to be submitted.

20. *The answers are:* (B) energy use reduction
    (D) sustainable site use
    (E) water use reduction

Remodeled projects typically achieve Building Reuse credits within the Materials and Resources credit category; however, they may have difficulty achieving credits in the Sustainable Sites, Water Efficiency, and Energy and Atmosphere categories. This is because when the site is predetermined, design teams do not have the opportunity to select a more favorable site that would help them achieve those credits. Compared to newer buildings, older buildings usually have less energy-efficient insulation systems, and have less efficient plumbing fixtures.

21. *The answers are:* (B) interior finishes
    (C) lighting
    (D) mechanical distribution

The LEED Core & Shell (CS) rating system is designed to help designers, builders, developers, and new building owners increase the sustainability of a new building's core and shell construction. It covers base building elements and complement the LEED for Commercial Interiors (CI) rating system. Interior space layout, interior finishes, lighting, and mechanical distribution may not be directly controlled by the developer, and therefore if a project team wishes to include these elements in their LEED certification, LEED CS may not be appropriate. Site selection and the building's envelope insulation can be directly controlled by the owner when pursuing LEED CS.

22. *The answers are:* (D) project administrators to manage LEED projects
    (E) project team members to manage LEED prerequisites and credits

LEED Online does not provide advertising of any sort. Project administrators assign access responsibilities for prerequisites and credits to project team members using LEED Online. Local code officials are unable to view online LEED documentation. The Energy Star Target Finder tool will help a project team analyze anticipated building energy performance.

23. *The answers are:* (A) Heat Island Effect

(E) Stormwater Design

Green roofs help mitigate stormwater and reduce the roof's heat island effect by increasing evapotranspiration (which has a cooling affect), and increasing the roof's albedo. Light pollution reduction is achieved through strategic lighting design. Site selection credit is achieved by not locating the building, or hardscapes, on the list of prohibited sites.

24. *The answer is:* (D) reduced toxic waste

Because mercury waste is toxic, using light bulbs with low mercury content, long life, and high lumen output will result in reduced toxic waste. Mercury content of lights does not affect light pollution, which refers to the impact of artificial light on night sky visibility.

25. *The answers are:* (A) light to night sky

(B) light trespass

(D) stormwater mitigation

Site lighting and stormwater mitigation must be addressed when designing a sustainable site. On-site renewable energy can reduce the building's burden on the power grid and is addressed in the Energy and Atmosphere category. Refrigerants affect ozone depletion and are addressed in the Energy and Atmosphere category.

While important, controlling light trespass and light to night sky are not prerequisites for sustainable site design.

26. *The answers are:* (B) evaluate durability risks of project

(C) incorporate durability strategies into design

The four basic elements of a durability plan are evaluation of durability risks; incorporation of durability strategies into design; implementation of durability strategies into construction; and complete a third party inspection of the implemented durability features.

27. *The answers are:* (A) ensure the technical soundness of the LEED reference guides and training

(C) resolve issues to maintain consistency across different LEED rating systems

Technical Advisory Groups (TAGs) respond to Credit Interpretation Requests (CIRs) and assist in the development of LEED credits. The Technical Scientific Advisory Committee (TSAC) ensures LEED and its supporting documentation is technically sound while assisting USGBC with complex technical issues.

28. *The answers are:* (B) preindustrial material

(C) rapidly renewable material

(D) regionally extracted material

The LEED EBO&M rating system defines the amount of material that must come from post-consumer, pre-industrial, rapidly renewable, or regionally extracted sources in order to earn credit for ongoing consumable purchases. The Rainforest Alliance certifies food, and is not related to ongoing consumables. Salvaged material use and purchase can contribute to earning credit for the sustainable purchases of durable goods and facility alterations, but not for ongoing consumables.

29. *The answer is:* (A) LEED CI

LEED for Commercial Interiors (CI) addresses tenant spaces within a building. Both LEED for New Construction & Major Renovation (NC) and LEED for Existing Buildings: Operations & Maintenance (EBO&M) are rating systems that apply to entire buildings. LEED for Core & Shell (CS) addresses buildings that are built with no, or limited, interior buildouts.

30. *The answer is:* (D) geographic location

USGBC chapters and regional councils identify which credits are eligible for Regional Priority points based on the needs of each environmental zone. LEED Online determines the region of a project based on its geographic location, which it identifies from the project site's zip code.

31. *The answers are:* (B) construction cost

(C) documentation cost

(E) soft cost

Project teams should consider the potential construction, soft, and documentation costs before committing to pursing a particular LEED credit. The application review cost is established regardless of the number or selection of LEED credits pursued, and is based on the building's floor area. Registration cost is the same for every LEED project, varying only depending on if the project is registered by a member or non-member company.

32. *The answer is:* (C) LEED EBO&M

Credit Interpretation Requests (CIRs) and appeals are components of every LEED rating system. LEED EBO&M is the only rating system that requires the implementation of performance periods.

33. *The answer is:* (D) ANSI/ASHRAE/IESNA 90.1-2007

ANSI/ASHRAE/IESNA 90.1-2007 sets minimum requirements for the energy-efficient design of all buildings except low-rise residential buildings. ANSI/ASHRAE 52.2-1999 addresses air cleaner efficiencies; ASHRAE 55-2004 addresses thermal comfort; and ANSI/ASHRAE 62.1-2007 addresses ventilation.

34. *The answers are:* (A) Controllability of Systems

(C) Indoor Chemical and Pollutant Source Control

Project teams intending to increase a building's ventilation will have to consider the implications on the building's commissioning, measurement and verification, and energy performance, all of which will be directly affected.

Controllability of Systems relates more to the thermal comfort and lighting of a building than the building's ventilation. Increasing ventilation will not help or prevent a project team from achieving Indoor Chemical and Pollutant Source Control.

35. *The answer is:* (B) track the movement of wood products from the forest to the building

A chain-of-custody document verifies compliance with Forest Stewardship Council (FSC) guidelines for wood products, which requires documentation of every movement of wood products from the forest to the building.

36. *The answers are:* (D) manufactured within 500 miles of the project site

(E) permanently installed on the project site

For the purposes of the LEED rating system, regional materials are those permanently installed building components that have been extracted, harvested or recovered, and manufactured within 500 miles of the project site.

Regional materials do not need to be recycled or post-consumer materials, nor do they need to be rapidly renewable (agricultural products that take 10 years or less to grow or raise and can be harvested in an ongoing and sustainable fashion). Forest Stewardship Council (FSC) certification applies only to wood and is not a requirement of regional materials.

37. *The answer is:* (C) Materials Reuse

A project team's choice of paint will have little or no effect on materials reuse. Choosing white exterior paint can contribute to reducing a building's heat island effect. Choosing paint with low volatile organic compounds (VOCs) will contribute to earning Low-Emitting Materials credit. Choosing bio-based paint can help a project team earn Rapidly Renewable Materials credit.

38. *The answers are:* (A) core credits

(C) innovation credits

(E) prerequisites

All LEED rating systems contain prerequisites, core credits, and innovation credits. Sustainable operations and educational programs may help a project team achieve either a core credit or an innovation credit.

39. *The answer is:* (B) door

Computers, office desks, and landscaping equipment are examples of durable goods, which are defined by the LEED reference guides as goods with a useful life of two years or more and that are replaced infrequently. Doors are considered part of the base building equipment.

40. *The answers are:* (C) local climate

(D) operational costs

Installing larger ventilation systems will minimally impact construction costs, but will significantly increase the energy cost throughout the life cycle of the building. Prior to increasing the ventilation rate of a building, the design winter and summer temperatures and humidity should be considered. Regardless of building location, the interior temperature should typically be between 68 and 74°F and the relative humidity should be between 50 and 55%. Refrigerant management is not affected by ventilation systems.

41. *The answers are:* (B) global warming potential

(C) ozone depletion potential

Refrigerants are chemical compounds that, when released to the atmosphere, deteriorate the ozone layer and increase greenhouse gas levels. LEED requires project teams to consider the ozone depletion potential and the global warming potential of refrigerants used in a building's HVAC & R system.

42. *The answers are:* (B) email address

(C) industry sector

(E) phone number

There is no cost to set up a personal user account on the USGBC website. The individual does not need to be a USGBC member, have prior LEED project experience, have or intend to have LEED credential, or supply his or her company name.

43. *The answers are:* (B) CIRs reviewed by a TAG for their own project

(D) CIRs posted prior to project application, for the applicable rating system only

Project teams are required to adhere only to CIRs uploaded to the USGBC website prior to project registration. Adherence is required for those submitted after project registration only if they were submitted by the project team itself. CIR requirements must be adhered to regardless of the project's geographic location; however, project teams are generally only required to follow CIRs for their specific rating system.

44. *The answers are:* (C) achieve the next incremental level of an existing credit

(D) double the requirements of an existing credit

Innovation in Design points for exemplary performance are earned for going above and beyond existing credit requirements. Alternatively, project teams can earn ID points for achieving the next incremental level of an existing credit if it is specified within the corresponding rating system.

45. *The answers are:* (B) collecting rainwater for sewage conveyance

(D) using cooling condensate for cooling tower make-up

As with every sustainable strategy, consult all applicable codes prior to implementation. Non-potable water used for cooling tower make-up and sewage conveyance can both lead to earning

LEED credit. On-site septic tanks do not reduce potable water used for sewage conveyance, and therefore do not contribute to the achievement of a LEED point for water conservation. Code requirements restrict project teams from using blackwater for landscape irrigation.

46. *The answer is:* **(C)** LEED credit equivalence submittal

Project teams intending to achieve Innovation in Design credit for innovation (not exemplary performance) must follow the LEED credit equivalence process, which requires the following.

- the proposed innovation credit intent

- the proposed credit requirement for compliance

- the proposed submittal to demonstrate compliance

- a summary of potential design approaches that may be used to meet the requirements

The Credit Interpretation Requests (CIRs) process does not involve the proposition of new credits, and therefore does not require an explanation of a proposed credit requirement. The LEED Online submittal templates do not allow for the proposal of new credits.

47. *The answer is:* **(B)** Center for Resource Solutions

The Center for Resource Solutions' Green-e energy program is a voluntary certification and verification program for renewable energy products.

Energy Star's Portfolio Manager is a federal program that helps businesses and individuals protect the environment through energy efficiency. The Department of Energy's mission is to advance the energy security of the United States. There is no such thing as the Center for Research and Development of Green Power.

48. *The answers are:* **(B)** International Energy Conservation Code (IECC)
                                (D) International Mechanical Code (IMC)
                                (E) International Plumbing Code (IPC)

The International Code Council (ICC) is a consolidated organization that comprises what was formerly the Building Officials and Code Administrators International, Inc. (BOCA), the International Conference of Building Officials (ICBO), and the Southern Building Code Congress International, Inc. (SBCCI). The ICC family of codes includes, but is not limited to, the International Building Code (IBC), the International Fire Code (IFC), the International Plumbing Code (IPC), the International Mechanical Code (IMC), and the International Energy Conservation Code (IECC).

49. *The answer is:* **(C)** Companies can be USGBC members.

People can be LEED-accredited, buildings can be LEED-certified, and companies (not individuals) can be USGBC members. It is not a requirement that a LEED project administrator (or anyone else involved with a LEED project) be a LEED AP.

50. *The answer is:* **(B)** 80%

A project team earning more than 40% but less than 50% of core credits within the LEED rating systems will earn a LEED Certified plaque. They will earn a LEED Silver plaque for earning more than 50% but less than 60% of Core Credits; LEED Gold for earning more than 60% but less than 80%; and LEED Platinum for earning more than 80%.

51. *The answers are:* **(C)** a means to submit a project for review

(E) the project's final scorecard

Project teams submit their projects to the Green Building Certification Institute (GBCI) for review using the LEED submittal templates, which also generate the final scorecard for LEED projects.

Project team members can manipulate the documentation for only those prerequisites or credits assigned to them. The LEED reference guides contain potential strategies for credit and prerequisite approval. Credit Interpretation Requests are reviewed and submitted at LEED Online, but not though submittal templates.

52. *The answers are:* **(A)** bid

(B) design

(D) pre-design

According to the *Sustainable Building Technical Manual*, an environmentally responsive design process includes the following key steps: pre-design, design, bid, construction, and occupancy. While the selection of vendors, consultants, and/or contractors is part of the process, it is not a key step. Re-bid and post-design should not occur if an appropriate process has been followed.

53. *The answer is:* **(C)** Projects can earn half points under the Site Selection credit.

LEED EB and LEED EBO&M projects must recertify at least every five years to maintain their LEED certification, but the LEED CI rating system does not have a recertification option. Precertification is only available if a project team is utilizing the LEED for Core & Shell rating system. Prohibiting smoking is an option in every LEED rating system for meeting the Environmental Tobacco Smoke prerequisite; because this is a prerequisite, no points are awarded for compliance.

54. *The answers are:* **(B)** clarify

(D) denied

(E) earned

An *earned* ruling requires no additional action from the project team. A *clarify* ruling requires the project team member to address the issues of the project reviewer. A *denied* ruling indicates that the project team member either misunderstood the intent and/or failed to meet the prerequisite or credit. Anticipated and deferred are ways to categorize prerequisites and credits reviewed during the design phase submittal.

55. *The answers are:* (A) delegate responsibility and oversee all LEED committee activities

(D) establish and enforce LEED direction and policy

The role of the LEED Steering Committee is to establish and enforce LEED direction and policy as well as to delegate responsibility and oversee all LEED committee activities.

Technical Advisory Groups (TAGs) respond to Credit Interpretation Requests and the GBCI develops and administers the accreditation exams. The Technical Scientific Advisory Committee (TSAC) ensures LEED and its supporting documentation is technically sound.

56. *The answers are:* (B) assign credits to project team members

(C) build a project team

(E) submit projects for review

Project administrators can do many things through the LEED Online workspace, including assigning credits to project team members, building the project team, and submitting projects for review. Previously submitted Credit Interpretations Requests (CIRs) can be viewed by USGBC company members as well as LEED project team members; however, credit appeals submitted by other project teams are not available for review. Precertification is a unique aspect of the LEED for Core & Shell rating system.

57. *The answers are:* (E) LEED for Homes rating system

(F) sample LEED submittal templates

(G) usgbc.org account

A free download of the LEED for Homes rating system is available at www.usgbc.org/homes. Sample LEED submittal templates are available at LEED Online. Individuals may create a free usgbc.org account.

All Credit Interpretation Requests (CIRs) require a fee be submitted to USGBC before a Technical Advisory Committee (TAG) will review it. The *LEED Reference Guide for Building Design and Construction* is available for purchase at **www.ppi2pass.com/LEED**. USGBC and LEED brochures are available for purchase at www.gbci.org/publications. LEED certification requires project registration, whose fees are described at www.usgbc.org/leedregistration.

58. *The answers are:* (A) additional response time may be incurred

(C) it is sent to the LEED Steering Committee

CIRs beyond the expertise of the Technical Advisory Group (TAG) are sent to the LEED Steering Committee and/or relevant LEED Committees for a ruling. Additional time is typically incurred in this situation.

59. *The answer is:* (A) LEED project tools

LEED project tools are only available to registered project teams. A directory of all LEED registered and certified projects, as well as posted rulings on Credit Interpretation Requests are available to registered USGBC members. LEED Online does not contain a list of LEED project credit appeals. While the project's submittal templates also become available after the project is registered, sample submittal templates are available to the public.

60. *The answers are:* (A) codes and regulations that address asbestos and water discharge

(B) codes and regulations that address PCBs and water management

Buildings must be in compliance with federal, state, and local environmental laws and regulations, including but not limited to those addressing asbestos, PCBs, water discharge, and water management. LEED certification can be revoked upon knowledge of noncompliance.

Complying with referenced standards that address sustainable forest management practices, fixture performance requirements for water use, and volatile organic compounds (VOCs) may help achieve LEED credits; however, doing so is not a they are not program requirement.

61. *The answers are:* (A) include members from varying industry sectors

(E) involve the team in different project phases

An integrated project team actively involves participants from varying industry sectors throughout the project, and meets monthly to review the project status.

The role of the commissioning authority is to verify the mechanical systems are operating as the designer intended. Product vendors may provide valuable insight that promoted the success of the project; however, they are not required on the project team. The purpose of including a LEED AP on a project team is to encourage LEED design integration and to streamline the application and certification processes, but including a LEED AP in not needed to create an integrated project team.

62. *The answer is:* (C) LEED EBO&M

Facilities undergoing minor envelope, interior, or mechanical changes must pursue LEED certification under the EBO&M rating system. Facilities undergoing major envelope, interior, or mechanical changes must pursue LEED certification under the NC rating system. LEED CI is used to certify tenant spaces while LEED CS is used to certify buildings prior to tenant infill.

63. *The answers are:* (D) use rainwater for sewage conveyance or landscape irrigation

(E) remediate contaminated soil

Soil remediation may help a project team achieve a credit under Brownfield Redevelopment, and using collected rainwater may earn a team points under the Water Efficiency category.

Erosion and sedimentation control, installing HCFC-based HVAC & R equipment, and the storage and collection of recyclables are LEED certification prerequisites (not credits).

64. *The answer is:* (D) To achieve LEED certification, every prerequisite and a minimum number of credits must be achieved.

The first step toward LEED certification is project registration. A fee must be paid when submitting Credit Interpretation Requests (CIRs). There is a LEED rating system for every type of building, including non-commercial buildings.

65. *The answer is:* (B) Optimize Energy Performance

Ground source heat pumps are energy efficient mechanical systems that may help project teams earn the energy performance prerequisite and credit. Ground source heat pumps contain a vapor compression refrigeration cycle, which requires electricity to operate, and therefore it is not a renewable source of energy. They do not generate energy (so they don't contribute to On-Site Renewable Energy credits), nor do they reduce the amount of water used by a project.

66. *The answers are:* (D) offer a volume certification path

                     (E) provide a streamlined certification process for large-scale projects

The goals of the Portfolio Program are to assist participants in integrating green building design, construction, and operations into their standard business practices using LEED technical standards and guidance; provide a cost-effective, streamlined certification path for multiple buildings that are nearly identical in design; recognize leaders who are creating market transformation through their commitments and achievements in green building; foster a network of investors, developers, owners, and managers committed to systemically greening their building portfolios; and support participating organizations in fulfilling their sustainability commitments by providing solid performance metrics that can be given to stakeholders.

Submittal templates provide a template of key data for the design team members to compile. The mission of LEED in general is to encourage and accelerate the "global adoption of sustainable green building and development practices through the creation and implementation of universally understood and accepted standards, tools, and performance criteria."

67. *The answers are:* (A) before the design phase

                     (B) during the construction phase

The LEED project budget should be addressed before the design phase and throughout the construction phase of the project. LEED project team selection is based on of the created budget.

68. *The answer is:* (C) installing native or adapted plants

Turf grass typically requires sizable amounts of water to sustain it, while native or adapted plants can survive on the amount of rainfall a site naturally receives. Projects with no landscaping are not eligible to earn landscaping credits. Invasive plants, such as weeds, are not considered landscaping by the LEED reference guides.

69. *The answer is:* (B) 4 points

Regionalization is an opportunity for project teams to earn additional points in the Innovation in Design category of each rating system. GBCI determines which six credits are priorities in each region of the US. Project teams in each region can earn up to four additional points for achieving the Regional Priority credits assigned to its region.

70. *The answer is:* (B) Energy Metrics

Energy Metrics credits focus on the building's energy performance and ozone protection.

Energy and Atmosphere is a credit category within the LEED rating systems, and is not a functional characteristic grouping. Materials Out credits are associated with the sustainable solid waste management policy of a building. Site Management credits address sustainable landscape management practices.

71. *The answers are:* (B) interior moisture loads

(D) pests

(E) ultraviolet radiation

The intent of durability planning is to appropriately design and construct high performance buildings that will continue to perform well over time. The principle risks are exterior water, interior moisture, air infiltration, interstitial condensation, heat loss, ultraviolet radiation, pests, and natural disasters.

72. *The answer is:* (B) contact a LEED for Homes provider

The first step for participating in the LEED for Homes program is to contact a LEED for Homes provider and then to register the project with GBCI. Becoming a LEED AP will strengthen your LEED knowledge; however, it is not required to pursue LEED certification in any rating system. Credit Interpretation Requests can be submitted only after a project is registered.

73. *The answer is:* (D) refrigerant leakage

HVAC & R equipment with a relatively short equipment life, a relatively high refrigerant charge, and/or refrigerant leakage will contribute to ozone depletion and global warming.

74. *The answer is:* (B) durability plan

As it is explained in the LEED for Homes rating system, a successful durability plan includes a ranking of durability risks and strategies to minimize the risks, which could include sealing ventilation ducts, installing rodent and corrosion-proof screens, and using air sealing pump covers.

The PE exemption form gives project teams the opportunity to follow a streamlined path to achieve certain prerequisites and credits. A building's landscape management plan focuses on ecology and wildlife outside of the building.

75. *The answer is:* (A) ASHRAE 55-2004

ASHRAE 55-2004 was created to establish acceptable indoor thermal environmental conditions. ANSI/ASHRAE 52.2-1999 addresses air cleaner efficiencies; ANSI/ASHRAE 62.1-2007 addresses ventilation; ANSI/ASHRAE/IESNA 90.1-2007 addresses building efficiency.

76. *The answers are:* (A) email address

(D) organization name

(E) individual's title

The primary contact of a LEED project is not required to be a LEED AP or have previous LEED project experience.

77. *The answers are:* **(D)** project summary

(E) project team members

The project team and project summary must be confirmed prior to the LEED application process. CIRs and precertification are items available for LEED project administrators; however, they are not required items. The project cost does not need to be confirmed prior to registration.

78. *The answer is:* **(A)** evapotranspiration

Evapotranspiration is the term used to describe water that is lost through plant transpiration and evaporation from soil.

79. *The answer is:* **(D)** view a protected electronic version of the LEED reference guide

An online reference guide access code is provided with the purchase of a LEED reference guide. The code provides its owner with electronic access to the reference guide. Project team members can also acquire the access code for 30 days of electronic access to the reference guide from a project team administrator after joining a LEED project.

80. *The answer is:* **(C)** intent

The structure of LEED prerequisites and credits is considered part of the LEED brand and includes intent, requirements, and potential technologies and strategies. This structure is maintained in each version of the LEED rating system. Economic and environmental benefits, greening opportunities, and submittal requirements are included in the rating systems and/ or LEED online.

81. *The answers are:* **(B)** durable goods

(E) waste stream

The environmental impact of refrigerants and energy consumption are addressed in the Energy and Atmosphere category. Materials and Resources credits address the flow of materials to and from a project site as well as the waste stream generated from a project building.

82. *The answer is:* **(D)** urban area

Building on a previously developed site helps conserve existing greenfields (undeveloped land). Locating a project in an urban location will provide the occupants with increased opportunities to utilize public transportation and reduce the need to drive to local amenities. LEED prohibits projects from building on public parkland, due to the potential economic and environmental implications.

83. *The answer is:* **(A)** declarant's name

Every LEED submittal template begins with the following statement: "I, *declarant's name*, from *company name* verify that the information provided below is accurate, to the best of my knowledge."

Product manufacturer info may be required for some documentation; however, it is not a requirement of every submittal. The project location is identified in the LEED registration form.

84. **The answers are:** (B) establishing a project budget

(C) establishing project goals

(D) site selection

The pre-design phase of every LEED project includes developing a green vision, project goals, priorities, building program, and budget; assembling a green team; developing partner strategies and project schedules; researching and reviewing local codes, laws, standards; and selecting a project site. Commissioning, testing and balancing, and training are steps of the construction phase.

85. **The answer is:** (A) CIRs must be submitted as text-based inquiries.

There is no mechanism available to submit attachments during the CIR process. A complete project narrative is not required, and the CIR is limited to 600 words.

86. **The answers are:** (D) energy efficiency

(E) environmental impact

(F) indoor environment

Green building design and construction should be guided primarily by energy efficiency, environmental impact, resource conservation and recycling, indoor environmental quality, and community considerations. Design and bid costs should be considered; however, green building focuses primarily on life-cycle costs. Construction documents are created once the guideline issues have been addressed.

87. **The answers are:** (A) accreditation of industry professionals

(C) certification of sustainable buildings

GBCI administers the LEED accreditation for industry professionals, and is responsible for the certification of buildings and parts of buildings. It does not certify products. USGBC provides sustainable education programs.

88. **The answers are:** (A) appeal

(D) construction

Credits can be earned during the construction phase of a project. Design credits can be submitted in the design review, but they will only be distinguished as "anticipated" or "denied." Project teams can modify a strategy and resubmit a design submittal credit in the construction phase to change the designation from "denied" to "earned". The construction review must include all design and construction credits that are pursued by the project team. After the construction review, credits are designated as "earned" or "denied." This designation can only be changed by submitting an appeal and paying a fee for each credit appealed. After the credit is appealed, it will be designated "earned" or "denied." The credit cannot be appealed a second time.

89. *The answers are:* (D) promotes design efficiency

                      (E) reduces design and construction time

Commissioning increases a project's initial cost, but should reduce its life-cycle cost. Commissioning authorities are not responsible for ensuring a project's compliance with a code. Rather, they verify that review design documents to help eliminate changes during construction or contractors from making design decisions. The commissioning agent's check helps prevent consultant re-design, as well as on-the-job engineering from the contractors, and therefore reduces the overall time spent on design and construction.

90. *The answers are:* (A) anthropogenic nitrogen oxide

                      (B) carbon dioxide

                      (D) sulfur dioxide

Conventional fossil-fuel generated electricity (such as that from coal-fueled power plants and liquid petroleum) results in the release of carbon dioxide into the atmosphere, which contributes to global warming. Coal-fired electric utilities emit both anthropogenic nitrogen oxide (nitrogen oxide that is a result of human activities, and which is a key contributor to smog) and sulfur dioxide (a key contributor to acid rain).

91. *The answer is:*   (D) shading hardscapes with vegetation

Heat island effect can be minimized by having high (not low) Solar Reflectance Index (SRI) values; minimizing the area of hardscapes; and shading necessary hardscapes with trees and bushes. The glazing factor is related to daylighting, not heat island effect.

92. *The answers are:* (B) indoor environmental quality criteria

                      (C) mechanical system descriptions

                      (E) references to applicable codes

Mechanical systems (which include HVAC & R, plumbing, and electrical systems) must be addressed in the Basis of Design (BOD). The BOD must also establish the procedure for the installed mechanical equipment to achieve the required indoor environmental quality criteria. Applicable codes must also be included to help provide guidance to the installing contractors. Process equipment and building materials may be addressed here; however, it is not a requirement.

93. *The answers are:* (B) energy sustainability consultant

                      (C) landscape architect

Utility managers, product manufacturers, and code officials may be a good resource for sustainability advice; however, they are not directly involved with the decisions of the project, and therefore are not considered part of the integrated project team.

94. *The answer is:*   (A) 50%

Replacement or upgrade to 50% of the building's envelope (walls, floors, and roof) is considered a major renovation. Replacement or upgrade to 50% of the building's interior (non-structural walls, floor coverings, and drop ceilings) is considered major. Replacement or upgrade to 50% of the building's mechanical systems (HVAC & R, lighting, plumbing) is considered major. The percentages are calculated using either the cost of the renovation or the area being renovated.

95. *The answer is:*   (B) 50%

Owners can occupy up to 50% of the building's leasable space and still be eligible to pursue LEED certification under the Core & Shell rating system. Buildings in which the owner occupies more than 50% of the leasable floor space must pursue LEED certification under the New Construction rating system.

96. *The answers are:* (A) Energy and Atmosphere

(F) Operational Effectiveness

Credits and prerequisites can be grouped by the credit categories designated within the LEED rating systems, or by functional characteristics. The Best Management Practices prerequisite falls within in the Energy and Atmosphere LEED credit category, but can also be grouped as an Operational Effectiveness prerequisite by its functional characteristic. Operational Effectiveness credits and prerequisites support best management practices.

97. *The answers are:* (B) gross area of the building

(D) project budget

(E) site conditions

The project's primary contact is the only individual required to submit their company's name. The project team creates a list of possible innovation strategies, which is submitted during the project application phase.

98. *The answer is:*   (B) previously certified under the LEED EBO&M rating system

LEED for Existing Buildings: Operations & Maintenance is the only rating system that has a recertification option available. Precertification does not exist for the LEED for Schools rating system.

99. *The answers are:* (C) installing heat recovery systems

(E) zoning mechanical systems

Increasing the ventilation rate and performing a flush out before occupancy improves indoor air quality but increases the amount of energy used. Reducing a building's heat island effect will not affect the building's energy use.

100. *The answer is:*   (D) VOC content in building materials

A building's indoor environmental quality can be improved by controlling noise pollution, providing as much natural lighting as possible, and providing adequate ventilation (thereby improving the air quality). Volatile organic compounds (VOCs), which damage lung tissue, should be minimized.

Practice Exam Two

1. Ⓐ Ⓑ Ⓒ Ⓓ Ⓔ
2. Ⓐ Ⓑ Ⓒ Ⓓ Ⓔ
3. Ⓐ Ⓑ Ⓒ Ⓓ
4. Ⓐ Ⓑ Ⓒ Ⓓ
5. Ⓐ Ⓑ Ⓒ Ⓓ
6. Ⓐ Ⓑ Ⓒ Ⓓ Ⓔ
7. Ⓐ Ⓑ Ⓒ Ⓓ Ⓔ
8. Ⓐ Ⓑ Ⓒ Ⓓ
9. Ⓐ Ⓑ Ⓒ Ⓓ
10. Ⓐ Ⓑ Ⓒ Ⓓ Ⓔ
11. Ⓐ Ⓑ Ⓒ Ⓓ Ⓔ
12. Ⓐ Ⓑ Ⓒ Ⓓ
13. Ⓐ Ⓑ Ⓒ Ⓓ
14. Ⓐ Ⓑ Ⓒ Ⓓ
15. Ⓐ Ⓑ Ⓒ Ⓓ
16. Ⓐ Ⓑ Ⓒ Ⓓ
17. Ⓐ Ⓑ Ⓒ Ⓓ
18. Ⓐ Ⓑ Ⓒ Ⓓ Ⓔ
19. Ⓐ Ⓑ Ⓒ Ⓓ
20. Ⓐ Ⓑ Ⓒ Ⓓ Ⓔ
21. Ⓐ Ⓑ Ⓒ Ⓓ
22. Ⓐ Ⓑ Ⓒ Ⓓ Ⓔ
23. Ⓐ Ⓑ Ⓒ Ⓓ
24. Ⓐ Ⓑ Ⓒ Ⓓ Ⓔ
25. Ⓐ Ⓑ Ⓒ Ⓓ Ⓔ

26. Ⓐ Ⓑ Ⓒ Ⓓ Ⓔ
27. Ⓐ Ⓑ Ⓒ Ⓓ
28. Ⓐ Ⓑ Ⓒ Ⓓ
29. Ⓐ Ⓑ Ⓒ Ⓓ
30. Ⓐ Ⓑ Ⓒ Ⓓ
31. Ⓐ Ⓑ Ⓒ Ⓓ Ⓔ Ⓕ
32. Ⓐ Ⓑ Ⓒ Ⓓ Ⓔ
33. Ⓐ Ⓑ Ⓒ Ⓓ Ⓔ Ⓕ
34. Ⓐ Ⓑ Ⓒ Ⓓ Ⓔ
35. Ⓐ Ⓑ Ⓒ Ⓓ Ⓔ
36. Ⓐ Ⓑ Ⓒ Ⓓ Ⓔ Ⓕ
37. Ⓐ Ⓑ Ⓒ Ⓓ
38. Ⓐ Ⓑ Ⓒ Ⓓ Ⓔ Ⓕ
39. Ⓐ Ⓑ Ⓒ Ⓓ Ⓔ
40. Ⓐ Ⓑ Ⓒ Ⓓ Ⓔ
41. Ⓐ Ⓑ Ⓒ Ⓓ
42. Ⓐ Ⓑ Ⓒ Ⓓ Ⓔ
43. Ⓐ Ⓑ Ⓒ Ⓓ Ⓔ Ⓕ
44. Ⓐ Ⓑ Ⓒ Ⓓ
45. Ⓐ Ⓑ Ⓒ Ⓓ Ⓔ
46. Ⓐ Ⓑ Ⓒ Ⓓ Ⓔ
47. Ⓐ Ⓑ Ⓒ Ⓓ Ⓔ
48. Ⓐ Ⓑ Ⓒ Ⓓ
49. Ⓐ Ⓑ Ⓒ Ⓓ
50. Ⓐ Ⓑ Ⓒ Ⓓ

51. Ⓐ Ⓑ Ⓒ Ⓓ Ⓔ
52. Ⓐ Ⓑ Ⓒ Ⓓ
53. Ⓐ Ⓑ Ⓒ Ⓓ
54. Ⓐ Ⓑ Ⓒ Ⓓ Ⓔ
55. Ⓐ Ⓑ Ⓒ Ⓓ Ⓔ Ⓕ
56. Ⓐ Ⓑ Ⓒ Ⓓ Ⓔ
57. Ⓐ Ⓑ Ⓒ Ⓓ Ⓔ
58. Ⓐ Ⓑ Ⓒ Ⓓ
59. Ⓐ Ⓑ Ⓒ Ⓓ
60. Ⓐ Ⓑ Ⓒ Ⓓ
61. Ⓐ Ⓑ Ⓒ Ⓓ
62. Ⓐ Ⓑ Ⓒ Ⓓ Ⓔ Ⓕ
63. Ⓐ Ⓑ Ⓒ Ⓓ Ⓔ Ⓕ
64. Ⓐ Ⓑ Ⓒ Ⓓ
65. Ⓐ Ⓑ Ⓒ Ⓓ
66. Ⓐ Ⓑ Ⓒ Ⓓ
67. Ⓐ Ⓑ Ⓒ Ⓓ
68. Ⓐ Ⓑ Ⓒ Ⓓ Ⓔ Ⓕ Ⓖ
69. Ⓐ Ⓑ Ⓒ Ⓓ Ⓔ
70. Ⓐ Ⓑ Ⓒ Ⓓ Ⓔ Ⓕ
71. Ⓐ Ⓑ Ⓒ Ⓓ
72. Ⓐ Ⓑ Ⓒ Ⓓ
73. Ⓐ Ⓑ Ⓒ Ⓓ
74. Ⓐ Ⓑ Ⓒ Ⓓ
75. Ⓐ Ⓑ Ⓒ Ⓓ Ⓔ

76. Ⓐ Ⓑ Ⓒ Ⓓ
77. Ⓐ Ⓑ Ⓒ Ⓓ
78. Ⓐ Ⓑ Ⓒ Ⓓ Ⓔ
79. Ⓐ Ⓑ Ⓒ Ⓓ
80. Ⓐ Ⓑ Ⓒ Ⓓ Ⓔ
81. Ⓐ Ⓑ Ⓒ Ⓓ
82. Ⓐ Ⓑ Ⓒ Ⓓ Ⓔ
83. Ⓐ Ⓑ Ⓒ Ⓓ Ⓔ
84. Ⓐ Ⓑ Ⓒ Ⓓ
85. Ⓐ Ⓑ Ⓒ Ⓓ Ⓔ Ⓕ
86. Ⓐ Ⓑ Ⓒ Ⓓ Ⓔ
87. Ⓐ Ⓑ Ⓒ Ⓓ
88. Ⓐ Ⓑ Ⓒ Ⓓ
89. Ⓐ Ⓑ Ⓒ Ⓓ Ⓔ

90. Ⓐ Ⓑ Ⓒ Ⓓ Ⓔ
91. Ⓐ Ⓑ Ⓒ Ⓓ Ⓔ
92. Ⓐ Ⓑ Ⓒ Ⓓ
93. Ⓐ Ⓑ Ⓒ Ⓓ
94. Ⓐ Ⓑ Ⓒ Ⓓ
95. Ⓐ Ⓑ Ⓒ Ⓓ Ⓔ Ⓕ
96. Ⓐ Ⓑ Ⓒ Ⓓ
97. Ⓐ Ⓑ Ⓒ Ⓓ
98. Ⓐ Ⓑ Ⓒ Ⓓ
99. Ⓐ Ⓑ Ⓒ Ⓓ
100. Ⓐ Ⓑ Ⓒ Ⓓ

1. What does a person need in order to to gain access to LEED online? (Choose two.)

    (A) access fee payment

    (B) project access code

    (C) corporate ID number

    (D) website password

    (E) website username

2. Collecting rainwater for sewage conveyance can help a project team achieve which of the following credits? (Choose three.)

    (A) Heat Island Effect

    (B) Innovative Wastewater Technologies

    (C) Site Development

    (D) Stormwater Design

    (E) Water Use Reduction

3. Mass transit options are generally more accessible to occupants of a building in an urban setting, and green roofs mitigate stormwater and reduce the heat island effect of buildings. Which LEED rating system category addresses mass transit, stormwater mitigation, and heat islands?

    (A) Energy and Atmosphere

    (B) Materials and Resources

    (C) Sustainable Sites

    (D) Water Efficiency

4. Which of the following describes the site area that is impacted by the building and hardscapes?

    (A) building footprint

    (B) carbon footprint

    (C) development footprint

    (D) project site

5. Which of the following steps should a project team NOT do before submitting a CIR?

    (A) Consult the applicable LEED reference guide.

    (B) Contact the TAG for guidance.

    (C) Review rulings on CIRs previously posted on the USGBC website.

    (D) Review the fee structure for the CIR submittal.

6. A project team can earn points for site selection by securing which of the following? (Choose two.)

    (A) access to public transportation

    (B) low microclimate factor

    (C) low VOC content of paints and coatings

    (D) parking availability

    (E) pedestrian access to basic services

7. Which of the following chemical compounds are commonly found in fire suppression systems and increase ozone depletion? (Choose two.)

    (A) chloroflourocarbons

    (B) halons

    (C) hydrofluorocarbons

    (D) VOCs

    (E) water

8. CIRs are collected _____ and rulings are posted _____ after receipt.

    (A) once each month; 12 business days

    (B) once each month; 25 business days

    (C) twice each month; 12 business days

    (D) twice each month; 25 business days

9. The LEED project registration form includes

    (A) a field for payment information

    (B) a streamlined path to achieve certain credits

    (C) an embedded calculator

    (D) an organizational strategy for document submittal

10. Which of the following items may contain VOCs? (Choose three.)

    (A) carpet systems

    (B) composite wood furniture

    (C) hardwood floors

    (D) linoleum floors

    (E) paints and coatings

11. The LEED NC, CI, and CS rating systems are organized into six environmental categories. Which of the following are categories within these LEED systems? (Choose three.)

    (A) Energy and Atmosphere

    (B) Innovation in Operations

    (C) Operational Effectiveness

    (D) Sustainable Sites

    (E) Water Efficiency

12. Which standard addresses building ventilation?

    (A) ANSI/ASHRAE 52.2-1999

    (B) ASHRAE 55-2004

    (C) ANSI/ASHRAE 62.1-2007

    (D) ANSI/ASHRAE/IESNA 90.1-2007

13. To minimize the impact refrigerants have on ozone depletion and global warming, project teams should select HVAC & R equipment with which of the following characteristics?

    (A) maximum refrigerant charge

    (B) minimal equipment life

    (C) minimal refrigerant leakage

    (D) minimal VOC content

14. An on-site wastewater treatment facility must accomplish which of the following objectives to achieve LEED credit?

    (A) meet the requirements of EPAct of 1992

    (B) send at least 20% of treated water to an underground aquifer

    (C) treat at least 50% of the project's wastewater

    (D) treat wastewater to secondary standards

15. Which of the following is a benefit of LEED CS precertification?

    (A) It provides a streamlined path for LEED CS certification.

    (B) It ensures LEED CS certification will be achieved.

    (C) It provides an opportunity to showcase the green features of the proposed building prior to construction.

    (D) It expedites the LEED plaque to the owner.

16. Rapidly renewable materials are materials that grow and mature within how many years?

    (A) 5 years

    (B) 10 years

    (C) 12 years

    (D) 15 years

17. Who is responsible for assigning roles to team members within LEED Online?

    (A) building owner

    (B) project administrator

    (C) project manager

    (D) project TAG

18. Which of the following can help a LEED project be completed within budget? (Choose three.)

    (A) avoid achieving LEED platinum certification

    (B) hire firms with numerous LEED Accredited Professionals

    (C) maintain documentation

    (D) monitor the LEED checklist throughout the project

    (E) perform energy/cost modeling as early as possible

19. To achieve LEED EBO&M certification, at least _____ of the project building's floor area must be _____.

    (A) 50%; leased

    (B) 50%; physically occupied for one year

    (C) 75%; leased

    (D) 75%; physically occupied for one year

20. Which of the following strategies will contribute to increasing occupants' access to natural light within a building? (Choose three.)

    (A) eliminating interior light shelves

    (B) increasing the amount of glazing

    (C) installing light-sensitive dimmers on all interior lights

    (D) installing skylights

    (E) reducing interior wall height

21. What is the first step toward LEED certification?

    (A) CIR submission

    (B) project registration

    (C) energy simulation model

    (D) application appeal

22. LEED submittal templates provide project teams with a means for doing which of the following? (Choose two.)

    (A) accessing rulings on CIRs

    (B) compiling key project information

    (C) communicating between team members and GBCI

    (D) confirming credit compliance

    (E) following a streamlined path to credits to bypass otherwise required submittals

23. Which of the following are NOT required to achieve an Innovation in Design credit?

    (A) credit intent

    (B) description of the product purchased for compliance

    (C) requirement for compliance

    (D) submittals necessary to demonstrate compliance

24. What is the role of the TAG? (Choose three.)

    (A) develop LEED accreditation exams

    (B) establish and enforce LEED direction and policy

    (C) maintain technical rigor and consistency in the development of LEED credits

    (D) respond to CIRs submitted by LEED project teams

    (E) review design phase credit submissions

25. Code officials may perceive light pollution reduction to be in conflict with which of the following? (Choose two.)

    (A) local nocturnal species survival

    (B) night sky visibility

    (C) site security

    (D) site safety

    (E) local government electricity cost

26. What is the role of the LEED Core Committees? (Choose two.)

    (A) assist USGBC with difficult technical issues

    (B) ensure the technical soundness of the LEED reference guides and training

    (C) recommend policies to the LEED Steering Committee

    (D) resolve issues to maintain consistency across different LEED rating systems

    (E) provide policy oversight to their relevant programs

27. Which of the following rating systems allows the owner to achieve LEED precertification?

    (A) LEED CS

    (B) LEED CI

    (C) LEED NC

    (D) LEED for Homes

28. A red exclamation point next to a credit name in LEED Online indicates that the credit is _____.

    (A) being pursued and no online documentation has been uploaded

    (B) complete and ready for submission

    (C) denied

    (D) not being pursued

29. Which is NOT true of the CIR process?

   (A) a project team can only submit five CIRs per project

   (B) CIRs are submitted online

   (C) the TAG's ruling does not guarantee credit achievement

   (D) the TAG's ruling provides clarification for both technical and administrative issues

30. Which of the following components is NOT required in a LEED EBO&M Policy Model?

   (A) applicable operations processes

   (B) performance measurement strategies

   (C) plans to increase policy awareness

   (D) list of teams and individuals involved in policy implementation

31. Which of the following are the key stages of an environmentally responsive design process? (Choose three.)

   (A) construction

   (B) occupancy

   (C) post-design

   (D) pre-design

   (E) re-bid

   (F) vendor selection

32. Which steps are involved in creating an integrated project team? (Choose two.)

   (A) conducting monthly progress meetings

   (B) selecting diverse team members

   (C) including at least one LEED accredited team member

   (D) registering the project early in the conception phase

   (E) reviewing previous rulings on CIRs

33. Once a project has undergone a design review, which of the following are potential rulings for each prerequisite and credit? (Choose two.)

   (A) anticipated

   (B) appealed

   (C) clarify

   (D) deferred

   (E) denied

   (F) earned

34. A building is undergoing a major renovation in which all fire doors will be recondi-
tioned to serve as plan tables. This strategy will help the project team achieve which
credit? (Choose two.)

     (A) Building Reuse

     (B) Construction Waste Management

     (C) Existing Building Commissioning

     (D) Materials Reuse

     (E) Regional Materials

35. Which of the following are considered natural refrigerants? (Choose two.)

     (A) hydrofluorocarbons

     (B) carbon dioxide

     (C) hydrocarbons

     (D) chloroflourocarbons

     (E) freon

36. The International Code Council (ICC) family of codes includes which of the following?
(Choose three.)

     (A) International Building Code

     (B) International Energy Conservation Code

     (C) International Fire Code

     (D) International Life Safety Code

     (E) International Registry Code

     (F) International Zoning Code

37. What information about the building owner must be provided for LEED project registration? (Choose two.)

     (A) account password

     (B) company name

     (C) corporate access ID

     (D) email address

38. Renovation of 50% of which of the following building components would be considered
a major renovation for the purpose of choosing the appropriate LEED rating system?
(Choose three.)

     (A) envelope

     (B) furniture and appliances

     (C) hardscapes

     (D) interior structural components

     (E) mechanical systems

     (F) walls and floors

39. What are the long-term benefits of commissioning? (Choose two.)

    (A) improved maintenance

    (B) improved operations

    (C) improved system performance

    (D) reduced ongoing commissioning cycle length

    (E) reduced operating cost of mechanical systems

40. Which of the following are renewable energy resources? (Choose two.)

    (A) ethanol

    (B) hydropower

    (C) natural gas

    (D) propane

    (E) uranium

41. Facilities undergoing major alterations and system upgrades CANNOT be certified under which rating system?

    (A) LEED CI

    (B) LEED CS

    (C) LEED EBO&M

    (D) LEED NC

42. Which of the following are considered principal durability risks? (Choose three.)

    (A) air infiltration

    (B) exterior water

    (C) heat loss

    (D) light pollution

    (E) visible transmittance

43. Which of the following are LEED certification levels? (Choose two.)

    (A) Certified

    (B) Bronze

    (C) Green

    (D) Precertified

    (E) Recertified

    (F) Silver

44. Which standard addresses mechanical ventilation system filters?

    (A) ANSI/ASHRAE 52.2-1999

    (B) ASHRAE 55-2004

    (C) ANSI/ASHRAE 62.1-2007

    (D) ANSI/ASHRAE/IESNA 90.1 -2007

45. Which of the following are considered innovative strategies within the LEED rating systems? (Choose three.)

    (A) implementing an educational outreach program

    (B) producing on-site renewable energy

    (C) reducing potable water use by 40%

    (D) using high volume fly ash concrete

    (E) using low-emitting furniture and furnishings

46. What phases should project team members be involved with to promote a LEED project's success? (Choose three.)

    (A) construction

    (B) energy analysis

    (C) final design

    (D) fund-raising

    (E) public support

47. Resource conservation credits can be achieved by doing which of the following? (Choose two.)

    (A) implementing a graywater irrigation system

    (B) reducing ventilation rates

    (C) using regional materials

    (D) using salvaged materials

    (E) using on-site photovoltaic panels

48. Once a project is registered, what must a project team submit through LEED Online?

    (A) construction documents

    (B) design documents

    (C) LEED certification level

    (D) project application

49. An individual _____ CANNOT create an account on the USGBC website.

    (A) who is no longer an employee of a USGBC member company

    (B) who is not a LEED AP

    (C) without an email address

    (D) without a LEED project access code

50. For the construction phase submittal of all desired credits, a project team is NOT required to submit which of the following?

    (A) documentation of design modifications for credits denied in the design phase

    (B) documentation of desired credits not submitted in the design phase

    (C) registration form with project scope and registration fee

    (D) verification that anticipated credit strategies have been implemented according to the design

51. There are five basic steps to follow when pursing LEED for Homes certification. Which of the following are considered basic steps? (Choose two.)

    (A) become a USGBC member company

    (B) build the home to the stated goals

    (C) create list of LEED-certified products to be used

    (D) identify the project team

    (E) precertify the project

52. Which of the following should be considered in a project's lighting purchasing plan?

    (A) mercury content

    (B) carbon content

    (C) VOC content

    (D) CFC content

53. A LEED project registration fee will be reduced if which of the following is true?

    (A) The building area is less than 50,000 sq ft.

    (B) The project is registered through a USGBC member company.

    (C) The project team intends only to earn a LEED Certified plaque.

    (D) The property area is less than 75,000 sq ft.

54. After which of the following phases can a project team earn LEED credits? (Choose two.)

    (A) CIR submission

    (B) construction phase

    (C) credit appeal

    (D) design phase

    (E) project registration

55. Which of the following are required for a building pursuing LEED certification under the LEED NC rating system? (Choose two.)

    (A) CIR submittal
    (B) commissioning
    (C) controlling ETS
    (D) having a LEED AP on the project team
    (E) precertification
    (F) using on-site renewable energy

56. A LEED for Homes project's durability plan would include the installation of which of the following? (Choose two.)

    (A) automatic humidistat controller
    (B) drain tile system at all footings
    (C) heat-recovery system certified by a LEED-approved testing lab
    (D) system for exhausting clothes dryers to the outdoors
    (E) water heating equipment with power-vented exhaust

57. Grouping LEED EBO&M credits by functional characteristics can provide a more logical approach to credit compliance. Which of the following are considered functional characteristics? (Choose two.)

    (A) Awareness & Education
    (B) Energy Metrics
    (C) Location & Linkages
    (D) Management Practices
    (E) Operational Effectiveness

58. Which of the following can improve the indoor environmental quality of a building?

    (A) diverting construction waste from disposal
    (B) maximizing acoustical control
    (C) minimizing refrigerant use
    (D) using on-site renewable energy

59. How often can a LEED EBO&M project recertify?

    (A) every six months
    (B) every year
    (C) every other year
    (D) every five years

60. The LEED EBO&M rating system includes a credit called Light Pollution Reduction. This credit would most likely fall under which of the following functional characteristic groupings?

    (A) Materials In

    (B) Materials Out

    (C) Operational Effectiveness

    (D) Site Management

61. One of the goals of LEED is to promote the selection of building sites where development will harm the environment the least. Building on which of the following sites would generally be described in the LEED reference guides as harmful to the environment?

    (A) brownfield

    (B) previously developed site

    (C) site in rural area

    (D) site located near a train station

62. Modifying which of the following can help a team achieve Daylight and Views credits? (Choose three.)

    (A) building commissioning

    (B) building orientation

    (C) site area

    (D) light pollution

    (E) occupant lighting control

    (F) sky lighting

63. Which of the following steps can be implemented during a project's design phase? (Choose two.)

    (A) commission mechanical systems

    (B) establish project budget

    (C) establish project goals

    (D) establish public transportation access

    (E) minimize use of CFCs in HVAC & R equipment

    (F) train maintenance staff

64. Which of the following people is NOT a necessary member of an integrated project team?

    (A) architect

    (B) landscape architect

    (C) mechanical engineer

    (D) property manager

65. Which of the following rating systems is most appropriate for the major renovation of a high school?

(A) LEED CS

(B) LEED EBO&M

(C) LEED NC

(D) LEED for Schools

66. Recycled content is defined in accordance with which of the following?

(A) Forest Stewardship Council

(B) Green Seal GS-11

(C) International Organization for Standardization

(D) Marine Stewardship Council Blue Eco-Label

67. Which of the following strategies is the LEAST likely to promote local ecosystem preservation?

(A) building on a brownfield site

(B) building on a previously developed site

(C) minimizing light pollution

(D) minimizing refrigerant use

68. Which of the following people are NOT responsible for documenting prerequisites and credits under the LEED EBO&M rating system? (Choose two.)

(A) architect

(B) building engineer

(C) commissioning authority

(D) groundskeeper

(E) facility manager

(F) owner

(G) property manager

69. Which of the following strategies can contribute to reducing the energy load of a building? (Choose two.)

(A) improving the building's envelope and glazing insulation

(B) installing on-site photovoltaic panels

(C) purchasing green-e power

(D) reducing the building's heat island effect

(E) reducing the building's lighting power density

70. Which of the following can influence the decision to use a particular LEED rating system instead of another? (Choose two.)

    (A) building size

    (B) project location

    (C) project type

    (D) project registration cost

    (E) project scope

    (F) rating system availability

71. Which of the following are described in the LEED reference guides as "the explanation of ideas, concepts and criteria created to promote the success of the project"?

    (A) basis of design

    (B) commissioning report

    (C) owner's project requirements

    (D) project narrative

72. What does the CIR process provide?

    (A) expedited credit reviews

    (B) guidance on LEED projects

    (C) pre-approval of credit submittal

    (D) strategies for LEED credit earning

73. Which of the following projects would be most likely to use the LEED NC rating system?

    (A) building project certified under the LEED NC rating system less than five years ago

    (B) new building project that will not be occupied by the owner

    (C) new high school building project

    (D) renovation of 60% of an owner-occupied building's envelope and mechanical systems

74. Installing a vapor retarder can result in which of the following?

    (A) limiting the disruption of natural hydrology

    (B) reducing the site's impervious cover

    (C) reducing water damage on a building's foundation

    (D) removing pollutants from stormwater runoff

75. Which of the following are included in the General Project Information section of the project registration form? (Choose two.)

    (A) project title

    (B) project address

    (C) project point total

    (D) project region

    (E) LEED rating system to be followed

76. Which of the following should a project team submit with a CIR?

    (A) credit name

    (B) letter of explanation

    (C) photographic examples

    (D) potential solutions

77. The role of the declarant is to _____.

    (A) register the LEED project

    (B) supply building materials to the LEED project team members

    (C) verify the content of a LEED credit through online documentation

    (D) review the LEED scorecard submitted by the LEED project team

78. Project teams can use which of the following non-potable water sources toward achieving a LEED credit for landscape irrigation? (Choose two.)

    (A) collected site rainwater

    (B) drip irrigation water

    (C) HVAC condensate

    (D) water from hose bibs

    (E) water used for sewage conveyance

79. In each LEED rating system, how many points can a project team earn from Regional Priority credits?

    (A) 2 points

    (B) 4 points

    (C) 6 points

    (D) 8 credits

80. Which of the following are NOT common environmental implications resulting from the use of natural gas, nuclear energy, and hydroelectric generators? (Choose two.)

    (A) depletion of fish populations

    (B) release of carbon dioxide

    (C) release of nitrogen oxide

    (D) sludge generation

    (E) waste transportation complications

81. Graywater typically CANNOT come from which of the following sources?

    (A) showers

    (B) stormwater runoff

    (C) toilets

    (D) washing machines

82. The LEED CI rating system can be used on which of the following renovation projects? (Choose two.)

    (A) five individual apartments within a residential building containing 10 apartments

    (B) five individual offices within a 60% owner-occupied building

    (C) individual office within multi-tenant building

    (D) individual retail store within a LEED CS-certified mall

    (E) walls and floors of all apartments within a three-story residential building

83. What should a LEED for Homes provider include in a preliminary review of a home's design? (Choose two.)

    (A) completed preliminary project checklist

    (B) project team member names

    (C) documentation of planned LEED education for designers and contractors

    (D) preliminary estimate of LEED for Homes score and certification level

    (E) preliminary evaluation of the LEED project registration fee

84. The purpose of a construction waste management plan is to _____.

    (A) achieve good indoor air quality during construction

    (B) increase the recycled material used to construct a building

    (C) reduce the amount of waste sent to landfills and incinerators

    (D) reduce the construction footprint

85. Green building design and construction should be guided by which of the following items? (Choose three.)

    (A) bid cost

    (B) community issues

    (C) construction documents

    (D) design cost

    (E) resource conservation

    (F) resource recycling

86. Which of the following can lead to achieving LEED CS credit? (Choose two.)

   (A) building on a brownfield site
   (B) fulfilling the prerequisites of the LEED NC rating system
   (C) increasing building ventilation
   (D) submitting a CIR
   (E) uploading the completed licensed professional exemption form

87. At least what percentage of credits must be achieved for a project team to earn LEED Silver certification?

   (A) 40%
   (B) 50%
   (C) 60%
   (D) 80%

88. Which of the following power sources generates sludge as a processing byproduct?

   (A) coal
   (B) hydroelectricity
   (C) nuclear power
   (D) petroleum

89. Certain prerequisites and credits require policy creation. Which of the following should be included in a policy model? (Choose two.)

   (A) goals
   (B) environmental benefits
   (C) financial implications
   (D) procedures and strategies
   (E) resources

90. Which of the following should a project team do before purchasing green power? (Choose three.)

   (A) choose green power options
   (B) create a green power procurement plan
   (C) create project plan for on-site installation of green power technologies
   (D) gather energy data
   (E) identify key decision makers

91. All LEED-certified buildings _____. (Choose two.)

   (A) are in the U.S.
   (B) conserve water
   (C) qualify for tax rebates
   (D) minimize greenhouse gas emissions
   (E) use renewable energy

92. What is the maximum percentage of a building's leasable space that an owner can occupy for a project to be eligible to pursue LEED CS?

    (A) 25%
    (B) 50%
    (C) 75%
    (D) 80%

93. Which of the following strategies could lead to a project team's earning a Sustainable Sites credit?

    (A) minimizing stormwater runoff
    (B) monitoring outdoor air delivery
    (C) using graywater for irrigation
    (D) using on-site renewable energy

94. Xeriscaping promotes which of the following?

    (A) water-efficient landscaping
    (B) reduced light pollution
    (C) reduced ozone depletion
    (D) community connectivity

95. Which of the following is NOT a prerequisite of the LEED CI, LEED NC, LEED CS, and LEED for Schools rating systems? (Choose two.)

    (A) Construction Activity Pollution Prevention
    (B) Fundamental Refrigerant Management
    (C) Minimum Acoustical Performance
    (D) Minimum Energy Performance
    (E) Storage and Collection of Recyclables
    (F) Water Use Reduction

96. Which of the following is described as a tool to help project teams track their credits against requirements for certification?

    (A) credit submittal templates
    (B) LEED Online
    (C) LEED rating systems
    (D) project checklist

97. Which of the following is NOT a basic element of designing a building for durability?

   (A) create an integrated design team
   (B) evaluate durability risks
   (C) incorporate durability strategies into construction
   (D) incorporate durability strategies into design

98. Can a project that is registered under an old version of a rating system upgrade to the current version of the rating system?

   (A) no, it must follow the version it was registered under
   (B) yes, but only for the LEED NC rating system
   (C) yes, if the project is in the design phase
   (D) yes, once the project becomes certified

99. Which of the following is true of all LEED NC- and CS-certified buildings?

   (A) 10% of the building is made from regional materials.
   (B) At least 50% of building occupants have access to daylight and views.
   (C) No refrigerants are used in HVAC & R equipment.
   (D) Water use is reduced compared to baseline water use conditions.

100. Every LEED AP credentialing process involves all of the following EXCEPT _____.

   (A) agreeing to disciplinary policies and credential maintenance guidelines
   (B) LEED AP application audit
   (C) passing the LEED Green Associate exam
   (D) professional experience on a LEED project

Practice Exam Two
Solutions

---

1. (A) (B) (C) ● ●
2. (A) ● (C) ● ●
3. (A) (B) ● (D)
4. (A) (B) ● (D)
5. (A) ● (C) (D)
6. ● (B) (C) (D) ●
7. ● ● (C) (D) (E)
8. (A) (B) ● (D)
9. ● (B) (C) (D)
10. ● ● (C) (D) ●
11. ● ● (C) (D) ●
12. (A) (B) ● (D)
13. (A) (B) ● (D)
14. (A) (B) ● (D)
15. (A) (B) ● (D)
16. (A) ● (C) (D)
17. (A) ● (C) (D)
18. (A) (B) ● ● ●
19. (A) (B) (C) ●
20. (A) ● (C) ● ●
21. (A) ● (C) (D)
22. (A) ● ● (D) (E)
23. (A) ● (C) (D)
24. (A) ● ● ● (E)
25. (A) (B) ● ● (E)

26. (A) (B) ● (D) ●
27. ● (B) (C) (D)
28. ● (B) (C) (D)
29. ● (B) (C) (D)
30. (A) (B) ● (D)
31. ● ● (C) ● (E) (F)
32. ● ● (C) (D) (E)
33. ● (B) (C) (D) ● (F)
34. (A) ● (C) ● (E)
35. (A) ● ● (D) (E)
36. ● ● ● (D) (E) (F)
37. (A) ● (C) ●
38. ● (B) (C) ● ● (F)
39. (A) (B) ● (D) ●
40. ● ● (C) (D) (E)
41. (A) (B) ● (D)
42. ● ● ● (D) (E)
43. ● (B) (C) (D) (E) ●
44. ● (B) (C) (D)
45. ● (B) (C) ● ●
46. ● ● ● (D) (E)
47. (A) ● (C) ● (E)
48. (A) (B) (C) ●
49. (A) (B) ● (D)
50. (A) (B) ● (D)

51. (A) ● (C) ● (E)
52. ● (B) (C) (D)
53. (A) ● (C) (D)
54. (A) ● ● (D) (E)
55. (A) ● ● (D) (E) (F)
56. (A) ● (C) ● (E)
57. (A) ● (C) (D) ●
58. (A) ● (C) (D)
59. (A) ● (C) (D)
60. (A) (B) (C) ●
61. (A) (B) ● ● (D)
62. (A) ● ● (D) (E) ●
63. (A) (B) (C) ● ● (F)
64. (A) (B) (C) ●
65. (A) (B) (C) ●
66. (A) (B) ● (D)
67. (A) (B) (C) ●
68. ● (B) ● (D) (E) (F) (G)
69. ● (B) (C) (D) ●
70. (A) (B) ● ● (D) ● (F)
71. (A) (B) ● (D)
72. (A) ● (C) (D)
73. (A) (B) (C) ●
74. (A) (B) ● (D)
75. ● ● (C) (D) (E)

76. (A) (B) (C) ■
77. (A) (B) ■ (D)
78. ■ (B) ■ (D) (E)
79. (A) ■ (C) (D)
80. (A) ■ (C) ■ (E)
81. (A) (B) ■ (D)
82. (A) (B) ■ ■ (E)
83. ■ (B) (C) ■ (E)
84. (A) (B) ■ (D)
85. (A) ■ (C) (D) ■ ■
86. ■ (B) ■ (D) (E)
87. (A) ■ (C) (D)
88. ■ (B) (C) (D)
89. ■ (B) (C) ■ (E)

90. ■ (B) (C) ■ ■
91. (A) ■ (C) ■ (E)
92. (A) ■ (C) (D)
93. ■ (B) (C) (D)
94. ■ (B) (C) (D)
95. ■ (B) ■ (D) (E) (F)
96. (A) (B) (C) ■
97. ■ (B) (C) (D)
98. (A) (B) ■ (D)
99. (A) (B) (C) ■
100. (A) ■ (C) (D)

1. *The answers are:* (D) website password

    (E) website username

Anyone with a USGBC website username and password can access LEED online. The LEED project administrator must provide you a project access code to be able to view and manage the documentation of a LEED project.

2. *The answers are:* (B) Innovative Wastewater Technologies

    (D) Stormwater Design

    (E) Water Use Reduction

Collecting rainwater for sewage conveyance reduces stormwater runoff and potable water usage.

Innovative wastewater technologies and Water Use Reduction both address plumbing fixtures used for sewage conveyance. Heat Island Effect addresses the solar reflectance of the site's building surfaces. Site Development addresses the open space percentage of the site.

3. *The answer is:* (C) Sustainable Sites

Sustainable Sites credits address building location as well as a building's impact on its immediate surroundings. Water Efficiency credits promote reduced demand for potable water, while Energy and Atmosphere credits aim to improve a building's energy performance, eliminate CFCs, and promote the use of renewable energy. Project teams seeking to achieve Materials & Resources credits will need to select sustainable materials and reduce mercury pollution and waste, and Indoor Environmental Quality credits promote the comfort and well-being of a building's occupants.

4. *The answer is:* (C) development footprint

Building structures, hardscapes, access roads, parking lots, and non-building facilities are included in the development footprint.

5. *The answer is:* (B) Contact the TAG for guidance.

The Credit Interpretation Request (CIR) submittal fee does not vary. Project teams should not contact the Technical Advisory Group (TAG) directly for guidance.

6. *The answers are:* (A) access to public transportation

    (E) pedestrian access to basic services

When selecting a site, the owner and/or developer should consider the availability of public transportation as well as pedestrian access to basic services (e.g., banks, restaurants, supermarkets, etc.). Strategic site selection can reduce the pollution created by private automobile usage and help project teams earn points for Alternative Transportation credits. Project teams do not earn points for providing parking for building occupants. It is desirable for a project to have a low microclimate factor, which contributes to a reduction in water use, but this affects the Water Efficiency credits, and not site selection. The volatile organic compound (VOC) content of paints and coatings does not factor into site selection.

7. *The answers are:* (A) chloroflourocarbons

    (B) halons

Halons, chlorofluorocarbons and hydrochlorofluorocarbons have a negative impact on the environment by increasing ozone depletion, so a building's fire suppression system should be designed with alternative suppressants. Water and hydroflourocarbons have no effect on ozone. Volatile organic compounds (VOCs) are generally found in paints, coatings, and adhesives, not in fire suppression equipment.

8. *The answer is:* (C) twice each month; 12 business days

USGBC collects all submitted CIRs twice each month. They are then sent to the appropriate Technical Advisory Group (TAG). The TAG will post their ruling on the Credit Interpretation Request within 12 business days of receipt.

9. *The answer is:* (A) a field for payment information

The LEED Project Registration form includes a field for payment information. (Payment is required to register a project.) The Licensed Professional Exemption form provides a streamlined path to achieve certain credits. The LEED project team must determine the most efficient organizational strategy to submit documentation. LEED online submittal templates include embedded calculators for credit compliance.

10. *The answers are:* (A) carpet systems

    (B) composite wood furniture

    (E) paints and coatings

Volatile organic compounds (VOCs) are compounds that, at room temperature, contribute negatively to indoor air quality. VOCs may be present in a wide variety of products, including adhesives, sealants, paints, coatings, carpet and carpet pads, composite wood, and agrifiber products. Linoleum floors are an example of a rapidly renewable product that does not contain VOCs. While hardwood floors may not be a good choice for sustainability, they do not generally contain VOCs.

11. *The answers are:* (A) Energy and Atmosphere

    (D) Sustainable Sites

    (E) Water Efficiency

Innovation in Operations is a LEED category under the LEED Operations and Maintenance rating system. Operational Effectiveness is a functional characteristic grouping, not a credit category.

12. *The answer is:* (C) ANSI/ASHRAE 62.1-2007

ANSI/ASHRAE 62.1-2007 specifies minimum ventilation rates for acceptable indoor air quality. ASHRAE 52.2-1999 addresses air cleaner efficiencies; ASHRAE 55-2004 addresses thermal comfort; and ANSI/ASHRAE/IESNA 90.1-2007 addresses energy efficiency.

13. *The answer is:* (C) minimal refrigerant leakage

The impact HVAC & R systems have on ozone is minimized by maximizing the equipment life, minimizing the refrigerant charge, and minimizing leakage. Refrigerant charge is the amount of refrigerant within an HVAC & R system. The higher the refrigerant charge, the worse the equipment's potential effect will be on the environment. Volatile organic compounds (VOCs) are not generally found in HVAC & R equipment.

14. *The answer is:* (C) treat 50% of the project's wastewater

To achieve LEED credit, an on-site wastewater treatment facility must treat a minimum of 50% of all wastewater generated by the project to tertiary standards, and must retain treated water for use or infiltration on-site. This may not be allowed by the building codes in some areas. As with every sustainable strategy, consult applicable codes prior to implementation.

Water use and the EPAct of 1992 are related to Water Efficiency credits, and not wastewater treatment.

15. *The answer is:* (C) It provides an opportunity to showcase the green features of the proposed building prior to construction.

LEED for Core & Shell precertification neither commits the owner to certification nor ensures certification will be achieved. It simply recognizes the goals to achieve LEED for Core & Shell certification through preliminary design documentation review. LEED precertification is not LEED certification; therefore, the owner does not receive a plaque unless the certification process is completed and enough points are earned. Projects that achieve precertification do receive a certificate and a letter confirming precertification. The green features of the proposed building can be marketed to potential tenants and financiers prior to construction.

16. *The answer is:* (B) 10 years

Agricultural products from both fiber and animal sources that grow and mature within 10 years are considered rapidly renewable materials.

17. *The answer is:* (B) project administrator

The project administrator assigns roles to project team members using LEED Online. The project administrator might be the building owner; however, it is not required. The Technical Advisory Group (TAG) is only assigned if the team submits a Credit Interpretation Request. There is no such title as project manager within the LEED rating systems.

18. *The answers are:* (C) maintain documentation
   (D) monitor the LEED checklist throughout the project
   (E) perform energy/cost model as early as possible

Hiring a firm with numerous LEED APs will not necessarily result in a LEED project's meeting its budget. Though implementing the strategies to achieve LEED Platinum certification may cost more, if the project budget has been established with this goal, the project should be able to achieve platinum with no additional costs.

19. *The answer is:* **(D)** 75% physically occupied for one year

To pursue LEED EBO&M certification, at least 75% of the project building's floor area must be physically occupied for at least one year, with the building systems in normal operation during that time. A building that is leased but not occupied does not meet the occupancy requirement of the LEED EBO&M rating system. USGBC allows occupancy time weighting (e.g., a building that is 50% occupied for six months and then 100% occupied for six months is the equivalent of one year of 75% occupation).

20. *The answers are:* **(B)** increasing the amount of glazing
                         (D) installing skylights
                         (E) reducing interior wall height

Increasing the number of windows (glazing) and installing skylights are two of the most straightforward ways to increase occupant access to natural light. Reducing interior wall height allows natural light to pass to more areas of a room, thereby increasing the occupants' access to natural light.

Interior light shelves help distribute natural light throughout a room; therefore, eliminating them would actually decrease occupant access to natural light. Light sensitive dimmers increase a building's energy performance; however, it will not improve access natural light levels.

21. *The answer is:* **(B)** project registration

Project registration establishes a project team's contact with GBCI and allows access to the online templates and previously submitted Credit Interpretation Requests (CIRs). A CIR cannot be submitted until the project is registered. An application appeal can not occur until the application is reviewed. The energy model simulation should be performed early in the design stages; however, it is not the first step toward LEED certification.

22. *The answers are:* **(B)** compiling key project information
                         (C) communicating between team members and GBCI

LEED online submittal templates provide project teams with a means of communication with Green Building Certification Institute (GBCI) and other team members, as well as a means of compiling key project information.

All rulings on Credit Interpretation Requests can be viewed by LEED project team members and all employees of USGBC member companies on the USGBC website. The Licensed Professional Exemption Form allows a streamlined path to bypass required submittals. GBCI does not notify project teams of credit compliance using online submittal templates.

23. *The answer is:* **(B)** description of the product purchased for compliance

The project team must submit their Innovation in Design credit in a fashion similar to the submission of all other credits. Solely purchasing a product will not meet the requirements to earn Innovation in Design credits, and therefore product descriptions will not contribute to earning Innovation in Design credits.

24. *The answers are:* (B) establish and enforce LEED direction and policy

         (C) maintain technical rigor and consistency in the development of LEED credits

         (D) respond to CIRs submitted by LEED project teams

The LEED Steering Committee establishes and enforces LEED direction and policy. The GBCI develops and administers the accreditation exams. USGBC reviews all credit submissions with the support of independently contracted reviewers.

25. *The answers are:* (C) site security

         (D) site safety

Light pollution reduction should enhance the environment of nocturnal species as well as night sky visibility. Poorly designed site lighting systems may be detrimental to site security and safety. Carefully designed exterior lighting is intended to reduce costs, not increase them. Reducing a building's light pollution does not mean that the local government will have to increase the lighting provided, and therefore it should not increase a local government's electricity cost.

26. *The answers are:* (C) recommend policies to the LEED Steering Committee

         (E) provide policy oversight to their relevant programs

The LEED Core Committees include LEED Management, LEED Steering, Technical Scientific Advisory, Education, Horizontal Market, Vertical Market, Curriculum and Accreditation, and Marketing. The Technical Scientific Advisory Committee (TSAC) ensures LEED and its supporting documentation are technically sound while assisting USGBC with difficult technical issues. Core Committees have the primary role and responsibility for developing and implementing policy.

27. *The answer is:* (A) LEED CS

Precertification is a feature that is exclusive to the LEED for Core & Shell rating system. It provides formal recognition of a project's intention to achieve certification under the LEED for Core & Shell rating system. The building need not be completed when the project team applies for precertification, and precertification does not commit the project team to continuing with the certification process.

28. *The answer is:* (A) being pursued and no online documentation has been uploaded

A red exclamation point indicates that the credit is being pursued and has been assigned to a project team member; however, no documentation has been uploaded.

29. *The answer is:* (A) a project team can only submit five CIRs per project

There is no limit to the number of CIRs that a project team can submit.

Credit interpretation rulings do not guarantee credit achievement; the project team must correctly design, install, and document the strategy to receive the credit. CIRs are submitted online and can provide clarification for technical and (though rarely) administrative issues.

30. *The answer is:* (C) plans to increase policy awareness

LEED EBO&M Policy Models must highlight the scope, performance metric, goals, procedures and strategies, responsible party, and time period. *Scope* includes a description of the facility management and operations processes applicable to the policy. *Performance metric* includes the team's intended strategies to measure the policy's performance. *Responsible party* includes teams and individuals involved in the policy's implementation.

31. *The answers are:* (A) construction

(B) occupancy

(D) pre-design

An environmentally responsive design process includes the following key stages: pre-design, design, bid, construction, and occupancy. Vendor selection, as well as consultant and/or contractor selection, is part of the process; however, it is not a key step. Re-bid and post-design should not be necessary if the process has been correctly established and implemented.

32. *The answers are:* (A) conducting monthly progress meetings

(B) selecting diverse team members

To successfully create an integrated project team, the team must be diverse and there must be monthly progress meetings to update the team on the project status and actively involve everyone throughout the project. Neither early project registration nor CIR review is necessary for a project team to be integrated. Project teams do not need to include a LEED AP.

33. *The answers are:* (A) anticipated

(E) denied

After a design review is conducted, each prerequisite is labeled as either "anticipated" or "denied". If a credit is anticipated, the construction team knows to build (or continue building) as designed. If a credit is denied, the consultants know to re-design in order to meet the prerequisite or credit requirements. No prerequisites or credits are awarded after the design review. Credits and prerequisites are officially earned only after the construction review. Teams have the opportunity to appeal denied credits after the construction review, but the credits are not labeled as such prior to the appeal.

34. *The answers are:* (B) Construction Waste Management

(D) Materials Reuse

Reconditioning part of a building to serve a different function in the building contributes to materials reuse as well as diverting materials from the construction waste stream. Building reuse applies to building items that continue to be used in their original design intent. Regional materials apply to building items that are extracted and manufactured within 500 miles of the project site. Commissioning is not related to reusing a building's components.

35.   *The answers are:* (B) carbon dioxide

(C) hydrocarbons

Refrigerants that are environmentally benign to the atmosphere are considered to be natural refrigerants. Carbon dioxide, water, ammonia, air, and hydrocarbons (such as propane, butane, and ethane) are considered natural refrigerants.

Hydrochlorofluorocarbons (such as freon), hydrofluorocarbons, and chlorofluorocarbons are not natural refrigerants.

36.   *The answers are:* (A) International Building Code

(B) International Energy Conservation Code

(C) International Fire Code

The International Code Council (ICC) is a membership association founded by the Building Officials and Code Administrators International, Inc. (BOCA), the International Conference of Building Officials (ICBO), and the Southern Building Code Congress International, Inc. (SBCCI). The ICC family of codes includes, but is not limited to, the International Building Code (IBC), International Fire Code (IFC), International Plumbing Code (IPC), International Mechanical Code (IMC), and International Energy Conservation Code (IECC).

37.   *The answers are:* (B) company name

(D) email address

The project administrator will provide the account password and corporate access ID number when registering a LEED project. The owner needs to provide their name, email, and company (or organization) name.

38.   *The answers are:* (A) envelope

(D) interior structural components

(E) mechanical systems

Renovation of a building's site (including hardscapes), no matter how extensive, is not considered a major renovation by USGBC. Renovation of 50% of the building envelope, interior structural components, or mechanical systems is considered major renovation. While walls and floors are part of the building's interior structural components, if there are additional structural components that are not renovated, then this would constitute a renovation of less than 50% of the building's interior, and thus is not a major renovation.

39.   *The answers are:* (C) improved system performance

(E) reduced operating cost of mechanical systems

Some of the long-term benefits of commissioning include improved system performance and reduced mechanical systems operating costs.

The operations and maintenance of a building are not necessarily related to the commissioning process. The scope, size, and complexity of the mechanical systems dictate the length of the ongoing commissioning cycle.

40. *The answers are:* **(A)** ethanol

                       (B) hydropower

Renewable energy is energy generated from natural sources and that is naturally replenished. Wind power, water power (hydropower), solar energy, geothermal energy, and biofuels (including ethanol) are examples of renewable energy. Non-renewable energy includes fossil fuels (coal, petroleum, natural gas), nuclear energy (from uranium), and propane.

41. *The answer is:*   **(C)** LEED EBO&M

Facilities undergoing minor envelope, interior, or mechanical changes must pursue LEED certification using the EBO&M rating system. Facilities undergoing major envelope, interior, or mechanical changes could pursue certification under either LEED NC, LEED CI, or LEED CS.

42. *The answers are:* **(A)** air infiltration

                       (B) exterior water

                       (C) heat loss

The intent of durability planning is to appropriately design and construct high performance buildings. The principal risks are exterior water, interior moisture, air infiltration, interstitial condensation, heat loss, ultraviolet radiation, pests, and natural disasters.

Visible transmittance is related to the amount of light passing through a glazing surface (window). Higher visible transmittance levels yield better natural lighting. Light pollution is not a durability risk.

43. *The answers are:* **(A)** Certified

                       (F) Silver

The available certification levels of the LEED rating systems are Certified, Silver, Gold, and Platinum.

44. *The answer is:*   **(A)** ANSI/ASHRAE 52.2-1999

ANSI/ASHRAE 52.2-1999 addresses the performance characteristics of air cleaners ASHRAE 55-2004 addresses thermal comfort; ANSI/ASHRAE 62.1-2007 addresses ventilation; ANSI/ASHRAE/IESNA 90.1-2007 addresses building efficiency.

45. *The answers are:* **(A)** implementing an educational outreach program

                       (D) using high volume fly ash concrete

                       (E) using low-emitting furniture and furnishings

Producing on-site renewable energy and reducing potable water use are strategies described by established credits. Exceeding the requirements of an existing credit is considered exemplary performance, not innovation. Innovative strategies are those that demonstrate quantifiable environmental benefits not already defined by the LEED credits. Innovative strategies can often be applied to a variety of LEED projects, but acceptance on one project does not automatically translate to approval on another project.

46. *The answers are:* (A) construction

                     (B) energy analysis

                     (C) final design

Gaining public support and fund-raising are owner and/or developer tasks. The project team should focus on the sustainable aspects of the project from conception to completion.

47. *The answers are:* (A) implementing a graywater irrigation system

                     (D) using salvaged materials

Within the LEED rating systems, building materials and water are considered resources; energy (use or production) is not. Though using regional materials may decrease the need for transportation (and therefore the amount of energy used and pollution generated), it is not considered a resource reduction strategy. Reducing ventilation rates will likely reduce energy usage (and indoor air quality), but does not contribute to resource conservation.

48. *The answer is:*   (D) project application

Before a project team can move forward, they must submit the application.

The LEED certification level is determined by the number of credits earned by the LEED project, after LEED certification, not during or application submission.

49. *The answer is:*   (C) without an email address

Anyone, regardless of LEED project experience, company membership, company type, or credentials can create a personal account on the USGBC website; however, the USGBC website's site user registration form requires that the registering individual have an email address.

50. *The answer is:*   (C) registration form with project scope and registration fee

If achievement of a particular credit is "anticipated," the project team must verify that the credit strategy has been implemented according to the design submittal. If a credit is "denied," the project team can either modify their implementation strategy and resubmit the credit in the construction phase, or opt to not pursue the credit. Credits that are not submitted in the design phase must be submitted in the construction phase.

Registration occurs prior to submitting the submittal templates for the design and construction phases.

51. *The answers are:* (B) build the home to the stated goals

                     (D) identify the project team

The five basic steps of the LEED for Homes certification process are as follows.

    1. Contact a LEED for Homes Certification provider and join the program.

    2. Identify the project team.

    3. Build the home to the stated goals.

4. Achieve certification as a LEED home.

5. Market and sell the home.

Becoming a USGBC member reduces the registration fee, but is not a basic step of LEED for Homes certification. Products are not LEED certified. Precertification is only possible for LEED Core & Shell projects.

52. The answer is: (A) mercury content

The lighting purchasing plan should specify the allowable limits of mercury content for all lights purchased for both the building and the associated grounds.

53. The answer is: (B) The project is registered through a USGBC member company.

The project registration fee is invariable unless a USGBC member company registers the project. In this case, there is a discount, which is described at www.usgbc.org/leedregistration.

54. The answers are: (B) construction phase

(C) credit appeal

Project teams can earn points after the construction phase and after the project team appeals a credit. Credits are never guaranteed after CIR submission or after design phase submittals. Credits are not granted upon project registration.

55. The answers are: (B) commissioning

(C) controlling ETS

All LEED NC projects must meet the fundamental commissioning and environmental tobacco smoke (ETS) prerequisites of the rating system. Submitting Credit Interpretation Requests (CIRs) is not required of any rating system. Project teams can earn points for having a LEED AP on the project team, or implementing an onsite renewable energy system, but these are not requirements. Precertification is only part of the LEED CS rating system.

56. The answers are: (B) drain tile system at all footings

(D) system for exhausting clothes dryers to the outdoors

A project's durability plan is part of the Innovation and Design process of LEED for Homes. It addresses issues that can degrade the materials of a home, such as moisture and pests. Automatic humidstat controllers, certified heat-recovery systems, and water heating equipment with power-vented exhaust are addressed by other sections of the LEED for Homes rating system.

57. The answers are: (B) Energy Metrics

(E) Operational Effectiveness

Energy Metrics credits focus on measurement of energy usage and ozone protection. Operational Effectiveness promotes reduced energy and water consumption. Location and Linkages and Awareness and Education are credit categories within the LEED for Homes rating system, not functional characteristics groupings within the LEED EBO&M rating system.

58. *The answer is:* (B) maximizing acoustical control

Indoor environmental quality includes light, noise, temperature, and air quality. While all of the strategies described can contribute to LEED project certification, only maximizing acoustical control will improve a building's indoor environmental quality.

59. *The answer is:* (B) every year

A project can recertify every year under the LEED EBO&M rating system. EBO&M projects must recertify at least once every five years to maintain their LEED certification.

60. *The answer is:* (D) Site Management

Site Management credits are site-specific and ensure sustainable maintenance and operations, including (but not limited to) light pollution reduction.

61. *The answer is:* (C) site in rural area

Locating the site in a rural location will promote additional transportation pollution from private automobile usage. Choosing previously undeveloped sites can disrupt existing greenfields and thus harm the environment. USGBC encourages building on brownfields and in urban centers that are accessible to public transportation.

62. *The answers are:* (B) building orientation
(C) site area
(F) sky lighting

The smaller the building area is in relation to the site area, the more access to daylighting the building in general, and thus the occupants will have. Strategic building orientation can maximize the amount of daylight in the building. Sky lighting increases daylighting and thus contributes to Daylight and Views credits. Commissioning is not related to daylighting; light pollution is related to lighting the night sky, not to daylighting; and allowing occupant lighting control contributes to achieving lighting controllability credits.

63. *The answers are:* (D) establish public transportation access
(E) minimize use of CFCs in HVAC & R equipment

Project teams can establish a plan for public transportation use and plan to minimize the use of CFCs in HVAC & R equipment in a project's design phase. The construction phase includes reviewing green products, testing proposed materials, building, and finally commissioning, testing, and balancing mechanical systems. The last step of construction is training. Establishing project goals and budgets are steps of the pre-design phase.

64. *The answer is:* (D) property manager

Property managers serve as the liaison between the tenant and the owner. A project can benefit from including property managers as part of the integrated project team; however, it is not a requirement.

65. *The answer is:* **(D)** LEED for Schools

Major renovations and newly built K-12 schools must follow the LEED for Schools rating system due to its emphasis on children's health. University academic buildings, K-12 athletic facilities, and interpretive centers are also eligible for the LEED for Schools rating system.

66. *The answer is:* **(C)** International Organization for Standardization

USGBC uses the International Organization for Standardization (ISO) to define recycled content. The Marine Stewardship Council Blue Eco-Label establishes guidelines for harvesting of seafood. The Forest Stewardship Council (FSC) addresses environmentally friendly forest management. Green Seal GS-11, *Green Seal Environmental Standard for Paints*, sets VOC limits for commercial flat and non-flat paints.

67. *The answer is:* **(D)** minimizing refrigerant use

USGBC encourages LEED project teams to avoid building on new sites and disturbing established ecosystems. To do so, they reward teams who build on brownfields (where there is generally no living species) and on previously developed sites. Light trespass from poorly designed outdoor lighting systems can affect nocturnal ecosystems on the site. While minimizing refrigerant use will help the global environment, it is less likely to have an immediate impact on local ecosystems.

68. *The answers are:* **(A)** architect

　　　　　　　　　　(C) commissioning authority

The declarants of prerequisites and credits in the LEED EBO&M rating system include the building engineer, the groundskeeper, the facility manager, the owner, and the property manager. There are no prerequisites or credits in the EBO&M rating system that require the architect or commissioning authority to act as declarant.

69. *The answers are:* **(A)** improving the building's envelope and glazing insulation

　　　　　　　　　　(E) reducing the building's lighting power density

Purchasing green-e power and installing on-site photovoltaic panels reduce the need for conventional power; however, they do not reduce the energy demands of the building.

70. *The answers are:* **(C)** project type

　　　　　　　　　　(E) project scope

The decision to choose a particular rating system can vary depending on project type and project scope. Varying project types include new construction, residential, tenant improvement projects, and so on. Project scopes range from entire building projects to major renovation projects, and so on. Some projects may qualify for more than one rating system. It is the responsibility of the LEED project team to determine the most appropriate rating system to follow.

Building size does not play a role in the decision-making process. For example, a major renovation of a 50,000 sq ft building or a 200,000 sq ft building will use the LEED NC rating system. Project registration cost is the same regardless of the rating system used. All LEED rating systems are uniformly available throughout the United States.

71. *The answer is:* (C) owner's project requirements

The owner creates the owner's project requirements (OPR) so that the designers can understand the vision for the desired building. The basis of design (BOD) is created to address the OPR. The commissioning authority reviews both and includes them in the commissioning report. The project narrative is what is included in LEED credit submittal process.

72. *The answer is:* (B) guidance on LEED projects

Rulings on Credit Interpretation Requests (CIRs) will answer the question asked by the project team, but will not provide a list of possible credit compliance strategies, or even alternative approaches to the one submitted. CIRs are optional, and are not directly involved in the credit review process. If a TAG approves a project team's strategy, this does not necessarily mean that the credit will be approved upon submittal.

73. *The answer is:* (D) renovation of 60% of an owner-occupied building's envelope and mechanical systems

A new building project that will not be occupied by the owner will most likely use the LEED for Core & Shell rating system. Buildings that were previously certified under the LEED for New Construction rating system are not eligible for recertification under the same rating system. A new high school building project should use the LEED for Schools rating system. Replacement or upgrade of 50% or more of a building's envelope, mechanical systems, or interior is considered a major renovation and should be registered under the LEED for New Construction rating system. LEED NC projects are generally owner-occupied.

74. *The answer is:* (C) reducing water damage on a building's foundation

The primary function of a vapor retarder is to prevent structural deterioration that can be caused by water trapped inside a wall, ceiling, or foundation materials. Disruption of natural hydrology is minimized by reducing impervious surfaces, increasing on-site stormwater infiltration and managing stormwater runoff. Constructed wetlands and vegetated filters are strategies that remove pollutants from stormwater runoff.

75. *The answers are:* (A) project title
(B) project address

The project point total is not determined until the LEED project team performs a design charrette and budgets are created. The rating system that will be pursued is selected in the Project Type section of the registration form. USGBC will determine the project's region based on the project's zip code.

76. *The answer is:* (D) potential solutions

The CIR process primarily helps project teams resolve technical questions, and sometimes helps them with administrative questions. The CIR must be submitted as a text-based inquiry with possible solutions. The CIR should not be submitted in a letter format with confidential project details since it will be made available for viewing by other LEED project teams. The credit name is automatically tracked, and the project team should not include it in their submission.

77. **The answer is:** (C) verify the content of a LEED credit through online documentation

The declarant is the LEED project team member who the LEED project team administrator assigns to document a credit. The declarant's title may or may not be specified, depending on the credit.

78. **The answers are:** (A) collected site rainwater
(C) HVAC condensate

HVAC condensate, collected rainwater, municipally supplied reclaimed water, and the project's graywater are all acceptable sources of non-potable water for landscape irrigation use. Water from drip irrigation and hose bibs is typically connected to the project's potable water distribution system. Water used for sewage conveyance is not clean enough to be used for irrigation.

79. **The answer is:** (B) 4 points

Project teams are eligible to earn up to four points for Regional Priority credits, which are based on regions in the U.S. The project zip code helps GBCI identify the project region.

80. **The answers are:** (B) release of carbon dioxide
(D) sludge generation

Natural gas is a major source of nitrogen oxide emissions. Nuclear power increases the potential for catastrophic accidents and raises significant waste transportation and disposal issues. Hydroelectricity plants disrupt natural water flows, resulting in disturbance of habitat and depletion of fish population. The rinsing process of coal generates sludge. Generating fossil-based electricity releases carbon dioxide.

81. **The answer is:** (C) toilets

Graywater is typically wastewater from domestic processes including laundry, dishwashing, and bathing. It can also come from collected stormwater runoff. Blackwater is wastewater from toilets and urinals. Reuse of graywater is significantly easier than that of blackwater, because it requires little or no treatment.

82. **The answers are:** (C) individual office within multi-tenant building
(D) individual retail store within a LEED CS-certified mall

Individual apartments are ineligible for LEED certification. The entire apartment building must pursue LEED certification. Project teams wanting to renovate a building's walls and floors must register for certification under the LEED for New Construction rating system. The owner can occupy a maximum of 50% of a building for the building to be eligible to pursue LEED Certification under the Commercial Interiors rating system.

83. *The answers are:* (A) completed preliminary project checklist

  (D) preliminary estimate of LEED for Homes score and certification level

The LEED for Homes provider's preliminary rating, which establishes how many points the home would have earned under the LEED for homes rating system before the home becomes a LEED project, must include a completed preliminary project checklist and a preliminary estimate of the LEED for Homes score and certification level. USGBC provides education for designers and contractors, and the builder must identify the project team members. The project registration fee does not vary from project to project.

84. *The answer is:* (C) reduce the amount of waste sent to landfills and incinerators

The construction waste management plan may actually increase the construction footprint (not reduce it) if additional dumpsters are required. An ideal plan will salvage materials from the waste stream for reuse within the building.

85. *The answers are:* (B) community issues

  (E) resource conservation

  (F) resource recycling

Green building design and construction should be guided by energy efficiency, environmental impacts, resource conservation and recycling, indoor environmental quality, and community issues. Design and bid costs should be addressed; however, green building focuses primarily on life-cycle costs. Construction documents are created once the guideline issues have been addressed.

86. *The answers are:* (A) building on a brownfield site

  (C) increasing building ventilation

LEED CS project teams can earn points for fulfilling the requirements of credits within that system. Since the prerequisites of the LEED NC rating system are identical to those of the LEED CS rating system, the team would not earn points for fulfilling these prerequisites. The licensed professional exemption form can only be used under the LEED EBO&M program.

87. *The answer is:* (B) 50%

A project team earning between 40% and 50% of the LEED rating system's core credits will earn a LEED Certified plaque. They will earn a LEED Silver plaque for earning between 50% and 60% of core credits; LEED Gold for between 60% and 80%; and LEED Platinum for 80% or more.

88. *The answer is:* (A) coal

The process of rinsing soil and impurities from coal generates sludge.

89. *The answers are:* **(A)** goals

  (D) procedures and strategies

All policies should include goals as well as procedures and strategies. LEED project team members are encouraged to set high goals and work toward them. Actual achievement is not required for the policy to be approved. Within the procedures and strategies, project teams should create an outline for items that can be implemented to achieve the goals set by the policy.

90. *The answers are:* **(A)** choose green power options

  (D) gather energy data

  (E) identify key decision makers

When pursing green power the preliminary steps should always be the same. The first step is to identify the key decision makers. This step establishes objectives of the green power program and should include high-level decision makers who can effectively promote and contribute funds to the program. The next step, gathering energy data, allows the project team to determine where energy can be saved, how much green power is required, and evaluate the environmental impacts of the organization's electricity consumption. The last preliminary step, choosing green power options, is the process of determining the appropriate green power solution for the organization.

91. *The answers are:* **(B)** conserve water

  (D) minimize greenhouse gas emissions

All LEED rating systems have prerequisites that require water conservation and minimization of greenhouse gas emissions. Many LEED-certified buildings qualify for tax rebates, but the rebates are not guaranteed. There are LEED-certified buildings in Canada. Using renewable energy is not a requirement of the LEED rating systems, although its use is covered in a LEED credit.

92. *The answer is:* **(B)** 50%

Owners can occupy up to 50% of a building's leasable space and still pursue LEED for Core & Shell certification. Buildings in which the owner occupies more than 50% of the leasable floor space must pursue LEED for New Construction.

93. *The answer is:* **(A)** minimizing stormwater runoff

A sustainable site will reduce the amount of stormwater it sends to the stormwater conveyance system. Using graywater for irrigation will help a project team earn Water Efficiency credits. Using on-site renewable energy will contribute to earning Energy and Atmosphere credit. Indoor Environmental Quality credits deal with outdoor air delivery.

94. *The answer is:* **(A)** water-efficient landscaping

The goal of xeriscaping is to reduce or eliminate the need for landscape irrigation. Examples of xeriscaping include using rock gardens, vegetation that uses minimal water, and so on.

95. *The answers are:* (A) Construction Activity Pollution Prevention

(C) Minimum Acoustical Performance

Since building construction is minimal and the LEED CI rating system is for projects within already-built buildings, there is no construction activity pollution prerequisite within the LEED CI rating system. Minimum Acoustical Performance is a requirement only of the LEED for Schools rating system.

96. *The answer is:* (D) project checklist

The LEED project checklist helps project teams track their credits against requirements for certification. LEED Online is described as a place for administrators to build project teams, assign credits to team members, and submit credits to GBCI for review. The LEED rating systems are performance-based guidelines for the design, construction and operation of commercial and residential projects. The credit submittal templates are a tool to help project teams interpret prerequisites and credits within a rating system.

97. *The answer is:* (A) create an integrated design team

The four basic elements of a durability plan are the evaluation of durability risks; incorporation of durability strategies into design; incorporation of durability strategies into construction; and implementation of third party inspection of durability features.

98. *The answer is:* (C) yes, if the project is in the design phase

LEED project teams have the opportunity, regardless of rating system used, to upgrade to the most current version if the project is still in the design phase.

99. *The answer is:* (D) Water use is reduced compared to baseline water use conditions.

All LEED for New Construction and LEED for Core & Shell projects must meet minimum water use prerequisites defined by their respective rating systems. While project teams can fulfill the Fundamental Refrigerant Management prerequisite by eliminating the use of refrigerants in HVAC & R equipment, the LEED rating systems provide alternatives for prerequisite compliance in certain cases. The use of regional materials and access to daylight and views is covered by credits, not prerequisites, of these rating systems.

100. *The answer is:* (B) LEED AP application audit

To become a LEED AP, the individual must agree to the disciplinary policies of GBCI, which require the individual to be truthful and cooperative when dealing with GBCI. The LEED AP credential maintenance program requires thirty continuing education units, six of which must be from a program teaching the LEED rating system. Some (between 5% and 7%) applications may be audited. Documentation of professional experience on one LEED project must be provided to sit for the exam. Anyone becoming LEED AP must pass the LEED Green Associate exam, which is the first part of the LEED AP exam.